# Let's Learn About Arts and Crafts

by
Gaye Ruschen

illustrated by Tom Foster

Cover by Laura Seeley

Copyright © Good Apple, Inc. 1987

ISBN No. 0-86653-389-3

Printing No. 987654321

**GOOD APPLE, INC.**
**BOX 299**
**CARTHAGE, IL 62321-0299**

The purchase of this book entitles the buyer to reproduce student activity pages for classroom use only. Any other use requires written permission from Good Apple, Inc.

All rights reserved. Printed in the United States of America.

This book is
dedicated to

Ruth, my mother,
who was resourceful in
discovering materials,
developing methods
and encouraging me to try,

And to Loren and Ginny,
who gave me the chance
to put into practice
the instincts
my mother had.

# Table of Contents

**Learning About Arts and Crafts** ............................. 1
Activity Table ............................. 2
Helpful Hints for Teachers ............................. 3

**Drawing and Coloring** ............................. 6
Observed Drawing ............................. 8
Leaf Rubbings ............................. 12
Musical Masterpieces ............................. 14
Scribble Designs ............................. 15
Discovering Stencils ............................. 16

**Cut and Paste** ............................. 20
Scissor Safety ............................. 21
Fun with Scissors ............................. 21
Shuffling Shapes ............................. 24
Apple Easy ............................. 26
Sassy Cats ............................. 27
Fanciful Flock ............................. 29
Feathery Friends ............................. 31
"Up-Standing" Turkeys ............................. 33
Brightly Shining T.P. Rolls ............................. 35
Snowman Mobiles ............................. 37
Fluttering Flags ............................. 39
Lovely Lambs ............................. 41
Loop Flowers ............................. 42

**Painting** ............................. 44
Other Ways to Use Paint ............................. 45
Tones and Shades ............................. 46
Spongy Trees ............................. 48
Inky Spiderwebs ............................. 50
Frosty Fingers ............................. 52
Easy Christmas Wreaths ............................. 54
Bottoms-Up Butterflies ............................. 56

**Collage** ............................. 58
Things to Do with Seeds and Beans ............................. 59
Things to Do with Clay ............................. 60

# Learning About Arts and Crafts

Arts and crafts are not just "something extra"; they provide valuable, enjoyable teaching tools which give children ways to explore, grow and learn.

Arts and crafts activities can complement, reinforce, enhance and broaden learning experiences the teacher will provide for the children in the classroom by allowing them to use their imaginations and to become comfortable with new ideas and materials.

Arts and crafts also require children to exercise self-control, follow directions and use materials in appropriate ways (a drop of glue at a time instead of half a bottle). Art can also reinforce skills and concepts you are teaching—skills like counting, cutting, and gluing can be practiced during an art project.

Developmentally, art activities help the child grow in many areas:

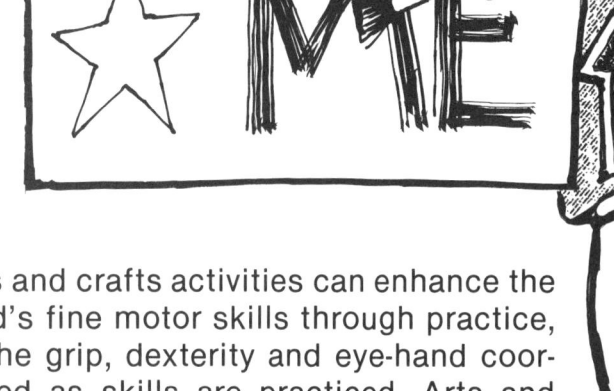

**GROSS MOTOR**
**VISUAL PERCEPTION**
**VOCABULARY**
**LISTENING SKILLS**
**SELF-CONCEPT**
**DECISION MAKING**

Most importantly, arts and crafts activities can enhance the development of the child's fine motor skills through practice, repetition and variety. The grip, dexterity and eye-hand coordination are all enhanced as skills are practiced. Arts and crafts activities can help children develop a larger naming vocabulary, establish better listening habits and provide countless hours of imaginative exercise and play.

The activities in this book are arranged so they will be convenient for teachers to use and beneficial for children to do. On the following page is a chart which tells which activities could be used at different times during the year. Teachers can use the chart to decide which projects will be most useful to them. Teachers should also feel free to add to, rearrange or add little special touches of their own to each project to make it more fun and exciting for their children.

# Activity Table

## FALL:

**September**
| | PG. |
|---|---|
| Leaf Rubbings | 12 |
| Apple Easy | 26 |
| Spongy Trees | 48 |

**October**
| | |
|---|---|
| Sassy Cats | 27 |
| Fanciful Flock | 29 |
| Inky Spiderwebs | 50 |

**November**
| | |
|---|---|
| Feathery Friends | 31 |
| "Up-Standing" Turkeys | 33 |
| Musical Masterpieces (Play "Over the River") | 14 |

## WINTER:

**December**
| | PG. |
|---|---|
| Brightly Shining T.P. Rolls | 35 |
| Easy Christmas Wreaths | 58 |
| Musical Masterpieces (Play *Nutcracker Suite*) | 14 |

**January**
| | |
|---|---|
| Snowman Mobiles | 37 |
| Frosty Fingers | 52 |
| Things to Do with Seeds and Beans (Use Popped Popcorn Kernels) | 59 |

**February**
| | |
|---|---|
| Fluttering Flags | 39 |
| Loop Flowers (See Other Suggestions) | 42 |
| Tones and Shades | 46 |

## SPRING:

**March**
| | PG. |
|---|---|
| Lovely Lambs | 41 |
| Musical Masterpieces (Play a Sousa march) | 14 |
| Scribble Designs | 15 |

**April**
| | |
|---|---|
| Loop Flowers | 42 |
| Things to Do with Seeds and Beans | 59 |

**May**
| | |
|---|---|
| Fluttering Flags | 39 |
| Spongy Trees (See Other Suggestions) | 48 |
| Bottoms-Up Butterflies | 56 |

## PROJECTS FOR ANYTIME:

| | PG. |
|---|---|
| Observed Drawing | 8 |
| Leaf Rubbings (See Other Suggestions) | 12 |
| Discovering Stencils | 16 |
| Fun with Scissors | 21 |
| Other Ways to Use Paint | 45 |

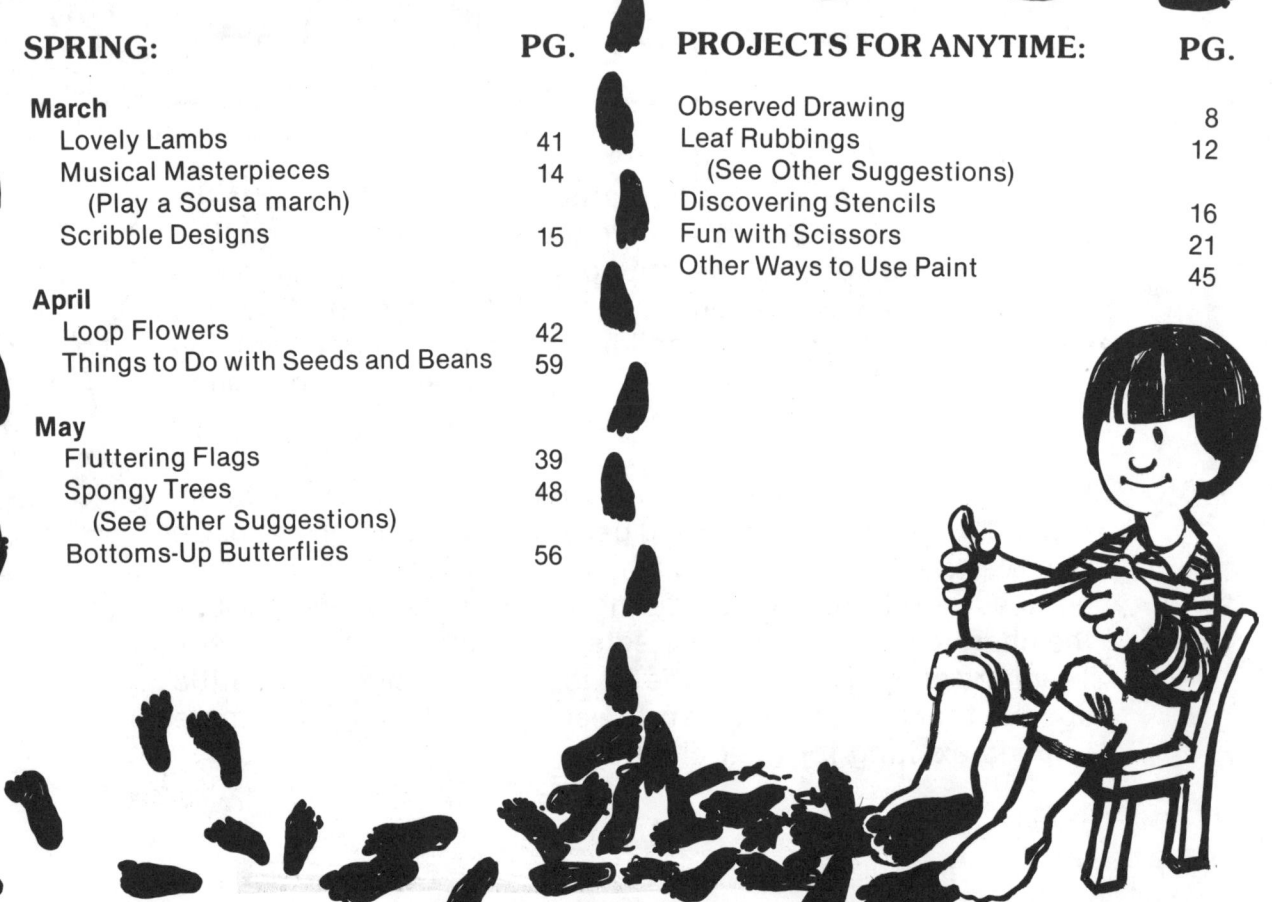

# Helpful Hints for Teachers

## DEVELOPING A GOOD ATTITUDE ABOUT ARTS AND CRAFTS

The attitudes children develop about certain subjects are often a reflection of what they see and hear from grown-ups. Here are some pointers for parents and teachers for developing a good attitude toward art projects for themselves and for the children they live and work with.

1. Accept children's artwork for what it is—works of art done by children!

2. Be encouraging and supportive. Let children discover what they like or don't like about colors, materials and methods for themselves.

3. Be open-minded and accepting. Enjoy the wonderful shapes, squiggles and creatures children can dream up.

4. Encourage children to do their best.

5. Be complimentary about "creations" children make. Don't compare or criticize what the children have worked so hard to make.

# Management

Try to be organized and as prepared as possible when you are planning an art activity. Plan your activity well ahead of time and prepare any materials you will need before you face the class with the project. Cut the paper into the sizes needed, mix the paint in the colors and thicknesses called for and try the project at least once by yourself. Don't be afraid to experiment with the directions you are given. Try to find the methods that you feel comfortable using and that will make the activity more enjoyable for your class.

Let the children do their own cutting, pasting and painting when they are able. Give specific instructions to them. Show an example of your work as you do the project; even if the children try to copy your work, they will still make something that is all their own. Observe and supervise the activity to make sure everything is running smoothly.

Watch for points of frustration among the children. Dull scissors that won't cut or a glue bottle that won't glue can be a major upset to a child. Step in to assist before the tears start to flow.

Provide a few simple ground rules for arts and crafts projects:

- Listen to directions!
- Keep materials at your work area.
- Share! (when necessary)

# Expectations

Don't assume that children know how to use arts and crafts materials properly or appropriately. Your idea of what is correct may be very different from that of their parents or former teachers. Also, remember many young children have not had the opportunity to use glue, paste, scissors or paint frequently until they enter a preschool or kindergarten setting.

Teach children how to use materials in a way that is acceptable to you. Provide them with opportunities to practice the methods you have taught them. Always try to emphasize the way to make something rather than what is being made.

## MOTIVATION

Provide some type of actual experience for the children before each project. Whether it is a field trip to a sheep farm, reading a story or popping corn in the classroom—provide some type of activity for the children that will be a springboard to the art activity. This introduction can be used to make the art project relate to another concept or skill area or can act as a transition between similar skills and concepts.

For each project you should make a list of ten questions that cannot be answered with a yes, no or one word. These questions can be used to get the children thinking about the particular skill or concept you are working on.

Asking the children questions about the project will keep them thinking during the entire process. They will make suggestions about how to do something or what to add to make the project better. Some of the ideas will be great, and you may want to write them down on the activities page for future reference.

# Drawing and Coloring

Drawing and coloring are activities most children come by naturally. Also most have had the opportunity to use crayons or pencils early in life. Because of this early exposure, teachers and parents should try to keep the use of crayons interesting. Here is a list of suggestions that might come in handy.

• Provide a variety of crayons for children to use at the art table or at the designated work area. Several types of crayons that you can collect or prepare are:

jumbo, large and regular crayons

crayons with and without paper

crayons shaped like cartoon characters, for example, Cabbage Patch Kids

muffin tin crayons—round, flat crayons that can be made by melting old crayons in the bottom of a muffin tin. Put baking papers in the bottom of the tins, break up the crayons into each tin and bake at 500° for 5 minutes. Make solid colors or rainbows!

• Vary the number of colors you provide once in awhile. One day put out only white crayons and dark paper, another day only black crayons and brightly colored paper. Some days put only different shades of the same color, etc. It may seem like a lot of work, but the children will look for a new and different "surprise" at the coloring corner each day!

• Not only should you vary the types of crayons you will use, you should vary the types of paper you use at the art table. Don't just use plain old manila paper all the time. Try cutting the manila paper into different sizes or into different shapes: hearts, eggs, trees, or geometric shapes. Use papers of different weights, colors and textures. Try using newspaper or tinfoil. Drawing will also reinforce many of the concepts presented in the activities of drawing and coloring, for example, color, design, shape, use of materials, etc. Creative drawing also allows the child to explore his imagination and to create something that is uniquely his own.

• You can also try this: To get children started on making drawings of their own, encourage them to "tell the story" first with a black crayon, marker or dark piece of chalk. When the child has completed the outline of his picture, he can start filling it in with colors of his choice to complete his drawing.

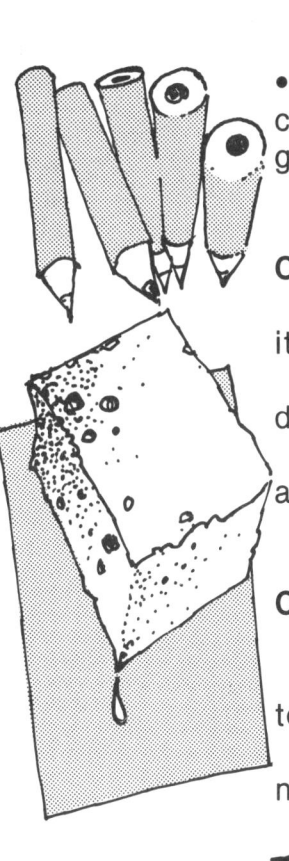

• Try using different types of materials, too. Use colored chalk, colored pencils, oil pastels and charcoal. Here are some suggestions for using each of these materials.

### COLORED CHALK

Make chalk drawings on the sidewalks or parking lots after it rains.

Wet the paper with a damp sponge before doing the chalk drawing.

Spray the paper with hair spray before drawing and spray it after to preserve the drawing.

### COLORED PENCILS

Use colored pencils instead of crayons to do rubbings.

Use colored pencils to color in the squares of graph paper to make a design.

Use colored pencils to practice writing letters, numbers, names, etc. Then decorate or illustrate them.

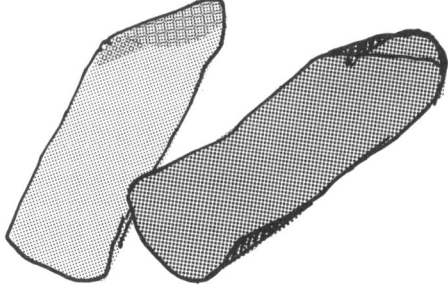

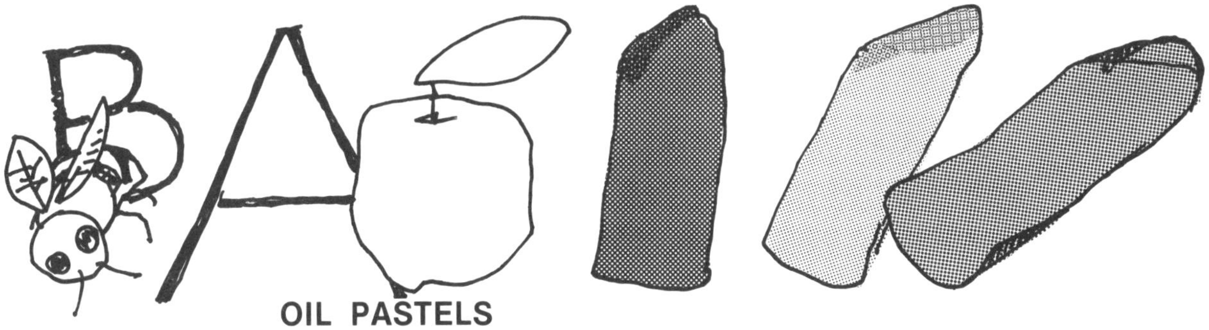

### OIL PASTELS

Let the children experiment with the pastels. Encourage them to use their fingers to smear and blend the colors.

Use different textures of paper (rough— manila, smooth— oaktag or ditto). Do the pastels behave differently on the different types of paper?

What new colors can you make by blending the pastels together?

Spray the pastel pictures with hair spray to keep them from smudging.

### CHARCOAL

Use charcoal on different colors of paper.

Smudge or blow the charcoal dust for a fuzzy effect.

Try doing rubbings with charcoal. Spray with hair spray to preserve. When the hair spray is dry, use markers, colored pencils or crayons to fill in the rubbings.

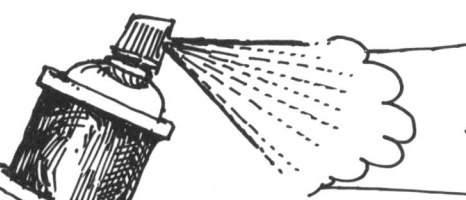
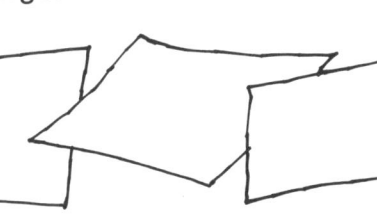
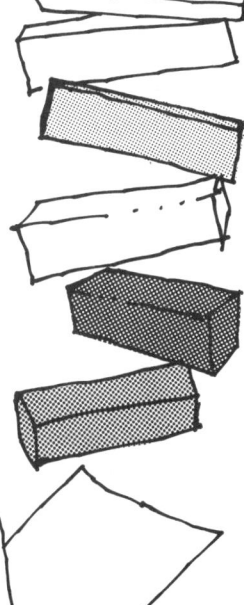

# Observed Drawing

Encourage the children in your class to draw from observation to balance the use of creative drawing and coloring and the use of coloring book activities in the classroom. Both types of activities can help improve the basic skills needed for arts and crafts activities and academic activities as well. Here are some suggested subjects to use for observed drawing.

- a favorite teddy bear or stuffed toy
- flowers and plants
- pieces of fruit or vegetables
- a stuffed animal or bird
- a classroom pet
- a classmate
- a piece of furniture—a chair or table
- a tree that can be seen from a classroom window
- a basket filled with items that go with a concept you are studying, for example, a basket filled with a toy rabbit, a raincoat, a rock and a rose while studying the sound that the letter *R* makes

## OTHER DRAWING ACTIVITIES

- Read a descriptive poem to the children like:

    "Mice" by Rose Fyleman
    "Every Time I Climb a Tree" by David McCord
    "I Like It When It's Mizzly" by Aileen Fisher
    "The Pirate Don Dirk of Dowdee" by Mildred Plew Miegs

Let them draw a picture of the character, animal, weather or mood that goes with the poem.

- Each day give the children a new topic to draw. Draw a picture of a place you would like to visit. Draw a picture of something you would like to get for your birthday.

- Make work sheets for the children that have one part of a creature drawn on it, such as an unusual and very curly tail, a pair of large mysterious eyes or a snout with whiskers and a long tongue. Several examples can be found on pages 9-11 and can be reproduced for use.

- The last two activities can also be used for language arts. Write a sentence describing what you have drawn.

## Draw a picture of the animal that belongs to this tail.

# Draw a picture of the creature that has eyes like this.

**Finish this creature.**

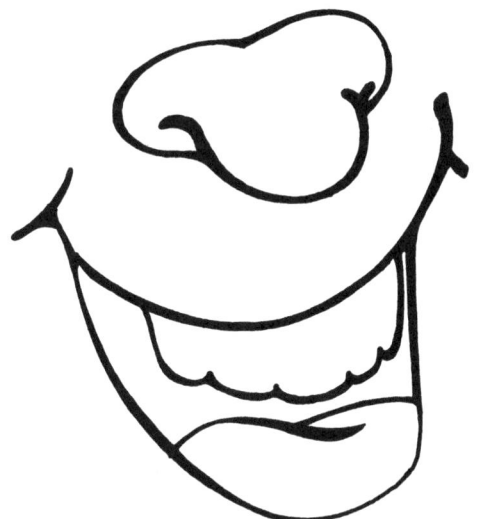

# Leaf Rubbings

**MATERIALS:**

- a collection of leaves—all sizes, shapes and varieties
- a lightweight paper (like ditto paper) in white or pastel colors
- crayons (with the paper removed)

**PROCEDURE:**

1. Show the children how to rub the crayon on its side. Make crayons and scrap paper available for them to practice the rubbing movement.

2. Show the children how to place the leaf under a piece of paper and how to rub the leaf across it. Once again let them practice this activity.

3. Place paper and a variety of leaves at each work area. Make sure you have plenty of extra paper available for the children to make more than one rubbing. Once they get started, they really enjoy watching the leaves magically appear.

4. Encourage the children to use different types of leaves and different colors on the same page. Also encourage the sharing of the different types of leaves between the children.

**OTHER SUGGESTIONS:**

- For a more active project to reinforce the concept of texture, let the children move around the room to discover as many different textures as possible, for example, cement block, cork, bark, floor tile, etc. Then let the children guess what their friends have rubbed.

- You can also make footprint rubbings by doing rubbings of the bottoms of the children's shoes. When this is done, let the children discuss the things that are alike and different about their shoes. Also let them discuss how they might discover what type of shoes a person wears by examining a rubbing of his shoe bottoms. Use this to broaden vocabulary skills as well as fine motor skills.

• Let the children make rubbings outside and at home. Bring them in to show them to the class. Can anyone guess what the rubbing is made from?

• Place several rubbings and the items from which they were made at a worktable. Let the children use the table as a learning center for matching. Can they match the rubbing to the correct object? Some ideas for making rubbings:
   coins (front and back sides)
   orange or grapefruit peels
   tree bark
   shoe bottoms with different textures
   the mesh of a baseball cap
   a wicker basket
Laminate these for repeated use.

• Make patterns with glue on pieces of tagboard. When they are dry, let the children make rubbings of them. The patterns can be doodles, numbers, letters, shapes or words.

• Let the children bring in items from home which they think would make good rubbings to add to the table.

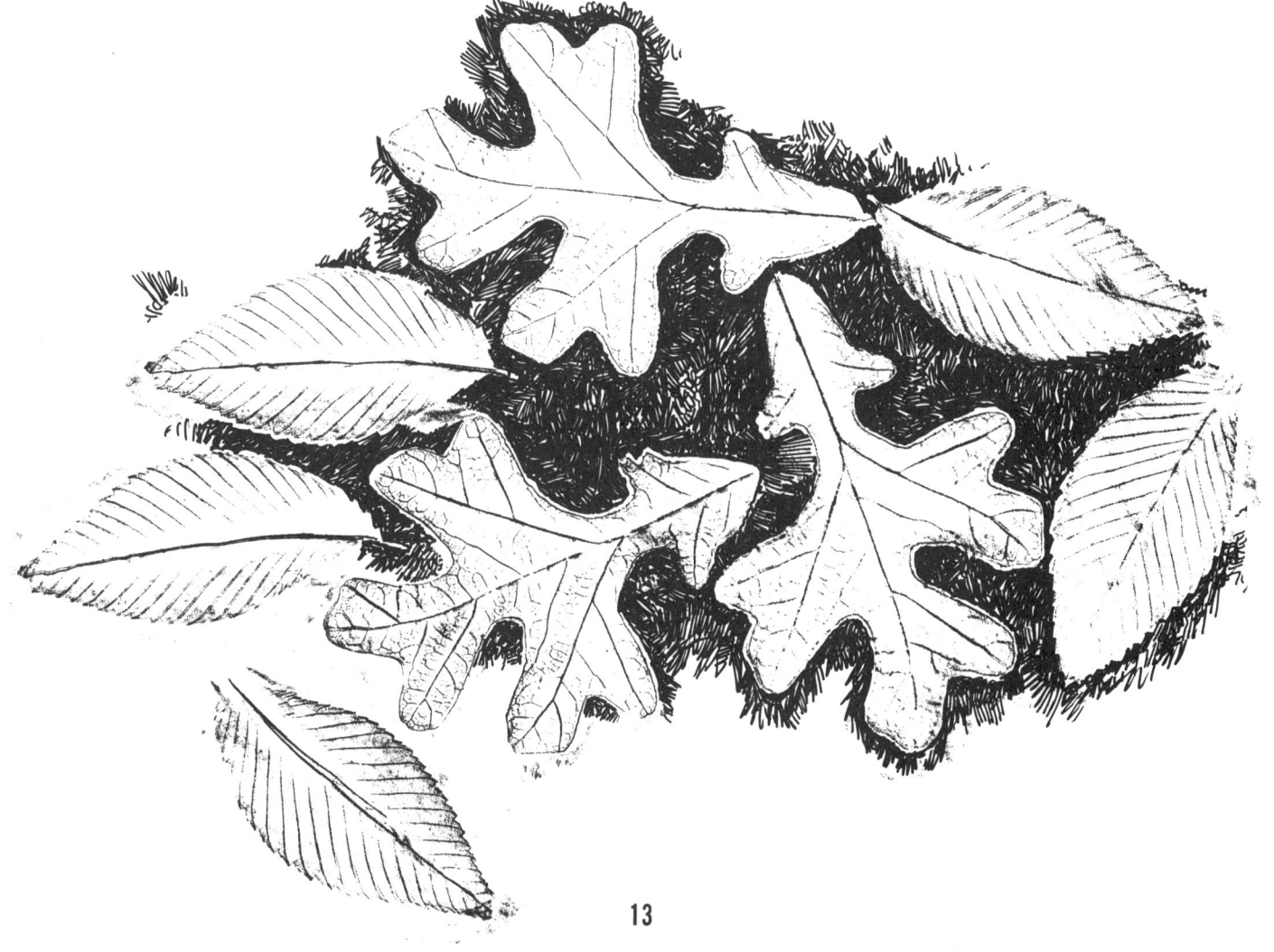

# Musical Masterpieces

**MATERIALS:**

- an expressive piece of instrumental music:
    *Peter and the Wolf*
    *Fantasy in Music*, Bomar Music
    *The Little Duck*, Anne Barlin

- large drawing paper, 9" x 18"

- crayons, markers or colored chalk or pencils

**PROCEDURE:**

1. Let the children listen to the record or tape you have chosen.
2. Discuss what they think the music is about, how it makes them feel, what colors it makes them think of, etc.
3. Pass out the drawing paper and the crayons, markers or colored chalk or pencils.
4. Listen to the piece again. Instruct the children to tell the story they have heard in the music by drawing the outline of the story with a dark colored crayon, marker or chalk.
5. Let the children fill the story they have just drawn with color.

**OTHER SUGGESTIONS:**

- For a language arts activity let each child tell the story of his picture to the class in a few sentences, or let him tell you about the picture he has made. Write the comments on the paper where they can be read by parents, teachers and other adults.

- Play different types of music:
    a march
    a lullabye
    a waltz

Tell the children to draw pictures of how the music makes them feel.

- Change the color of the paper. Change the shape of the paper. For instance, if using *The Little Duck* tape, give the children yellow paper that is egg-shaped.

# Scribble Designs

**MATERIALS:**

- 9" x 12" white construction paper
- glue in squeeze bottles. If you have purchased glue by the gallon, you may use old permanent solution bottles that have been well-washed and sterilized to prevent the children from making contact with toxic substances. If you know a beautician, she will probably be more than happy to save these bottles for you in a sack or box that you provide.
- colored chalk

**PROCEDURE:**

- Check the glue bottles to make sure they are full enough and the nozzle is clear in order for the glue to flow freely.

1. Demonstrate to the children how to squeeze the glue onto the white paper in a scribble pattern.
2. Pass out white paper and a bottle of glue to each child. Let the children dribble their own designs onto the paper you have given them.
3. Set the papers aside and let the glue dry.
4. After the glue has dried, use colored chalk to decorate the spaces between the dribbles. Encourage the children to share the different colors of chalk with one another.

**OTHER SUGGESTIONS:**

- Make crayon rubbings of the glue design after it has dried. Then you have the actual design to decorate and a "print" of it. Or trace a coloring book page with glue. Let it dry. Let the children make a rubbing of the page.

- Try adding India ink to the glue to make a dark outline.

- Try using black paper instead of white.

- Let the children practice drawing their shapes with glue. Color or decorate them when the glue has dried.

- Use poster paint to fill in the spaces. Add Kool-Aid or flavoring to the paint for an added touch the children will enjoy.

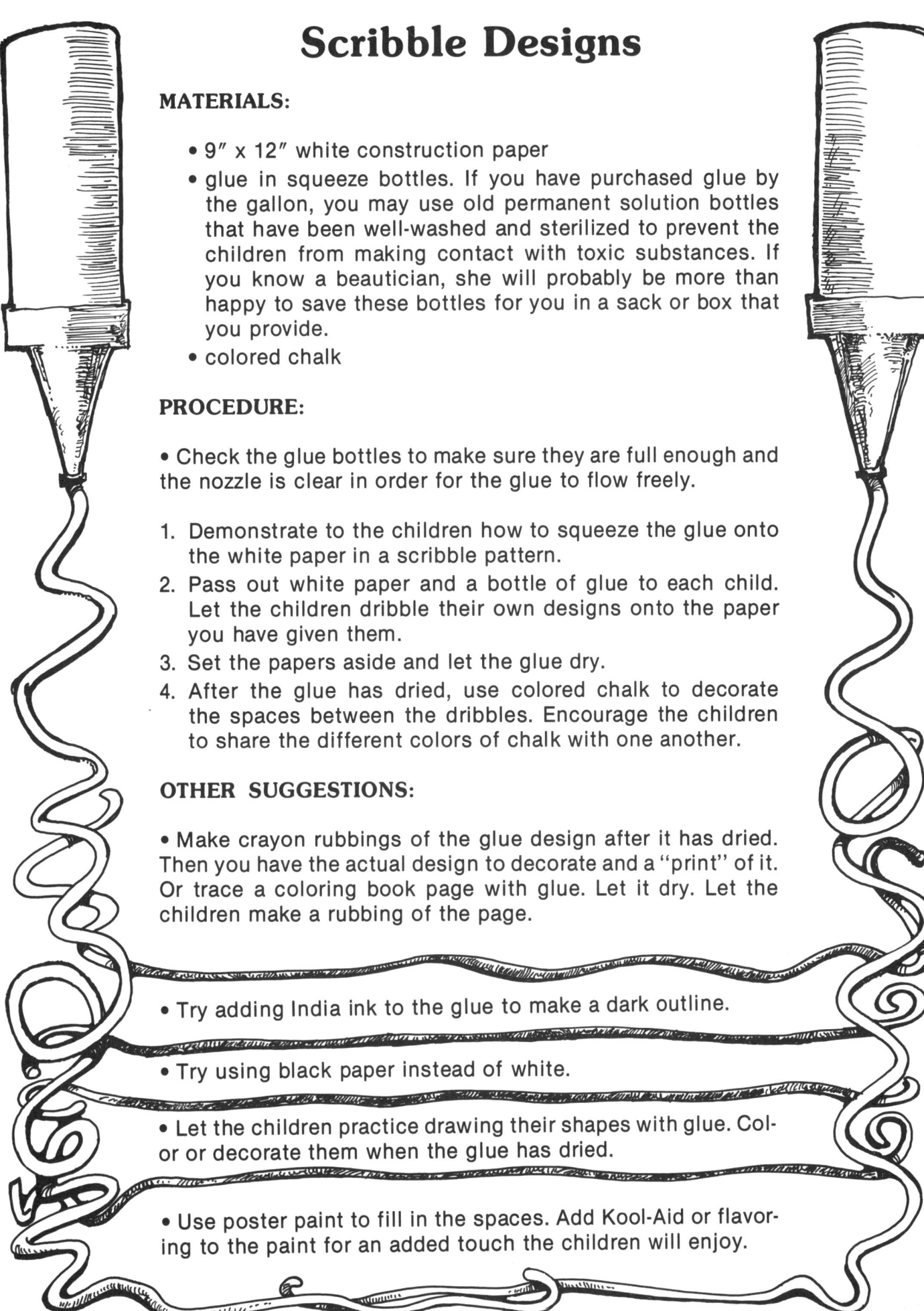

# Discovering Stencils

**MATERIALS:**

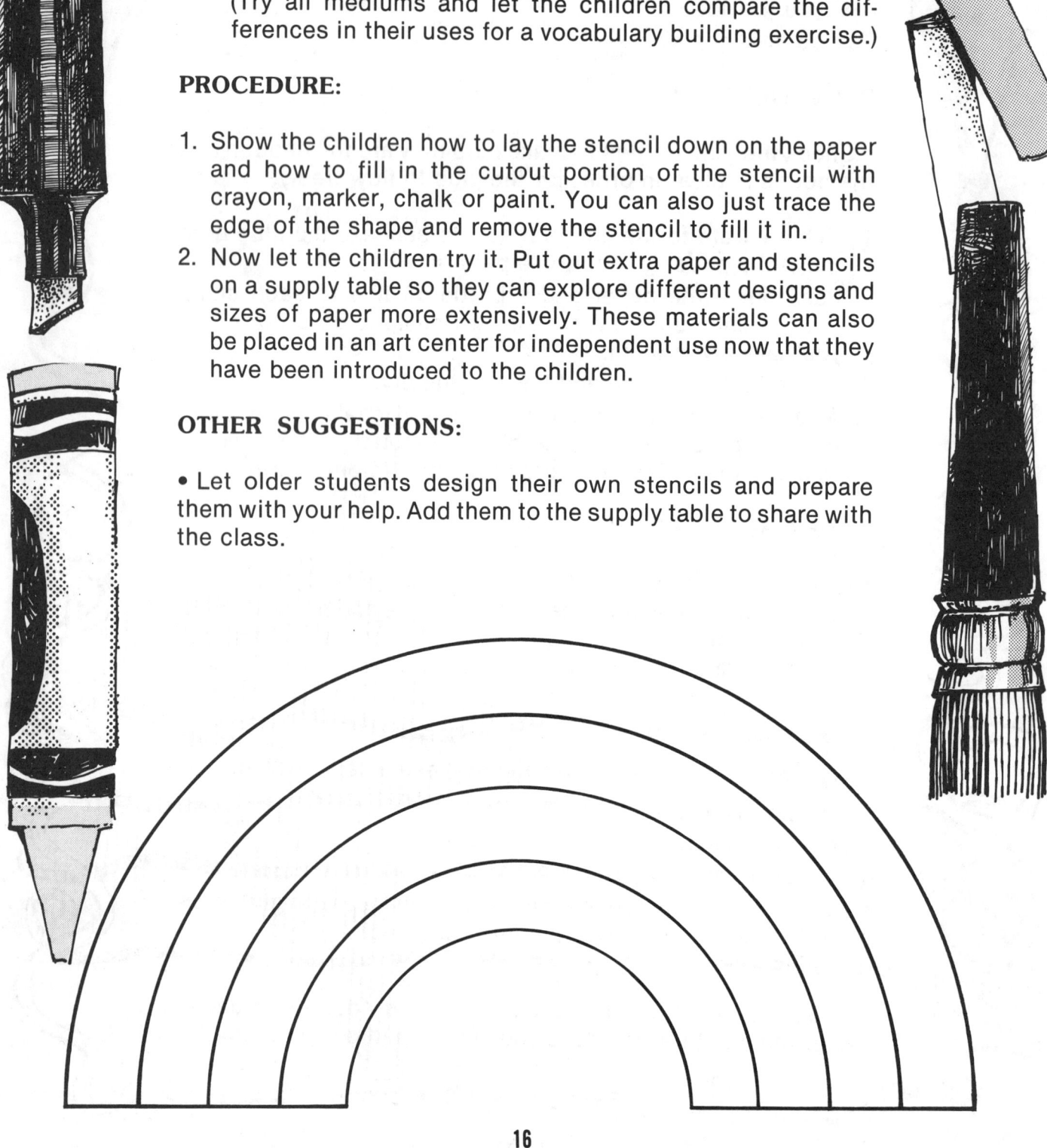

- a variety of stencils made from cardboard or mylar (a clear stiff plastic). Stencils are now available in most craft shops and can be purchased, or they can be made by tracing the design on cardboard or mylar and using an X-acto knife or razor blade.
- construction paper of different sizes, shapes and colors
- crayons, chalk, markers or paint can be used with stencils. (Try all mediums and let the children compare the differences in their uses for a vocabulary building exercise.)

**PROCEDURE:**

1. Show the children how to lay the stencil down on the paper and how to fill in the cutout portion of the stencil with crayon, marker, chalk or paint. You can also just trace the edge of the shape and remove the stencil to fill it in.
2. Now let the children try it. Put out extra paper and stencils on a supply table so they can explore different designs and sizes of paper more extensively. These materials can also be placed in an art center for independent use now that they have been introduced to the children.

**OTHER SUGGESTIONS:**

- Let older students design their own stencils and prepare them with your help. Add them to the supply table to share with the class.

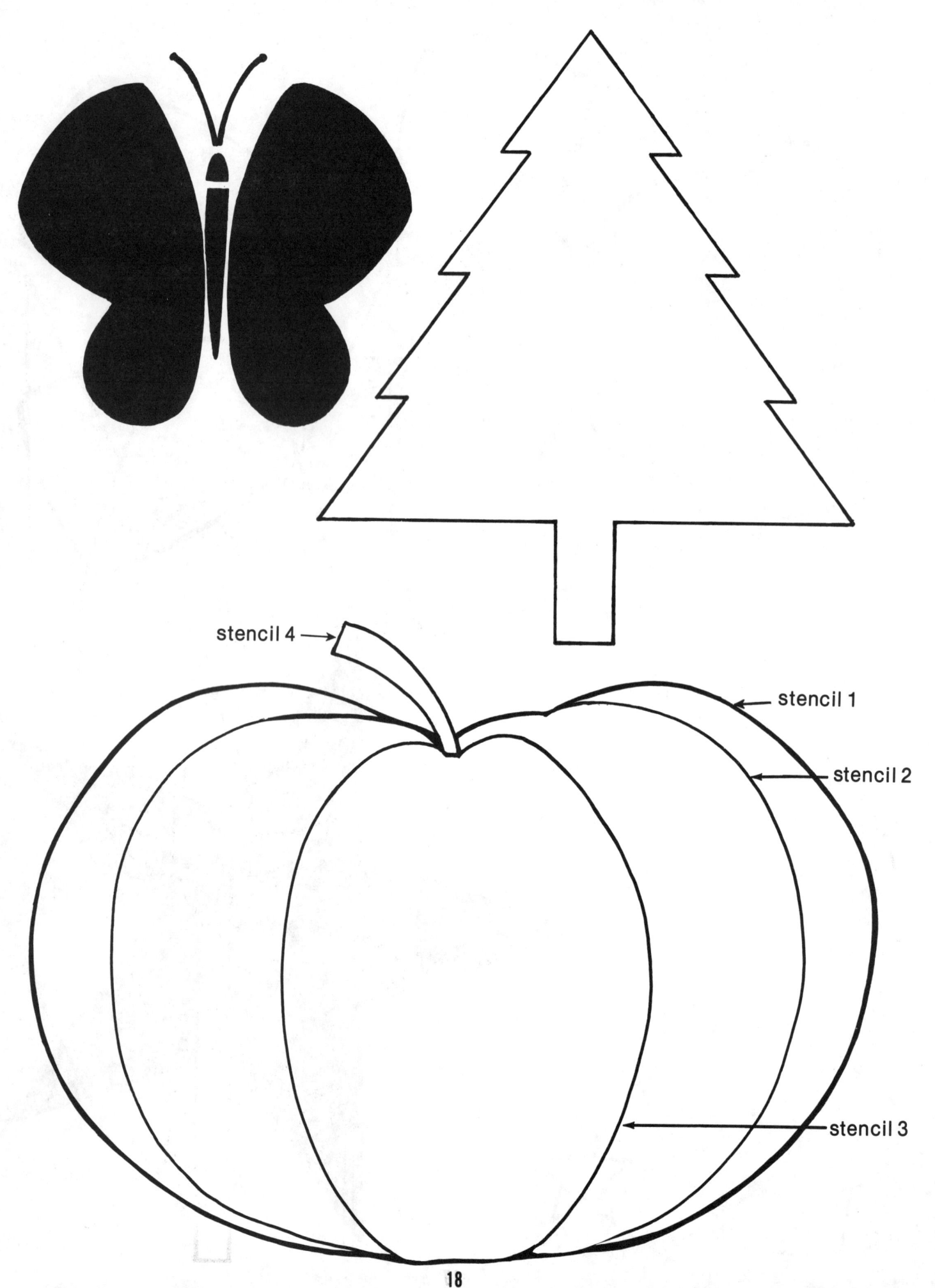

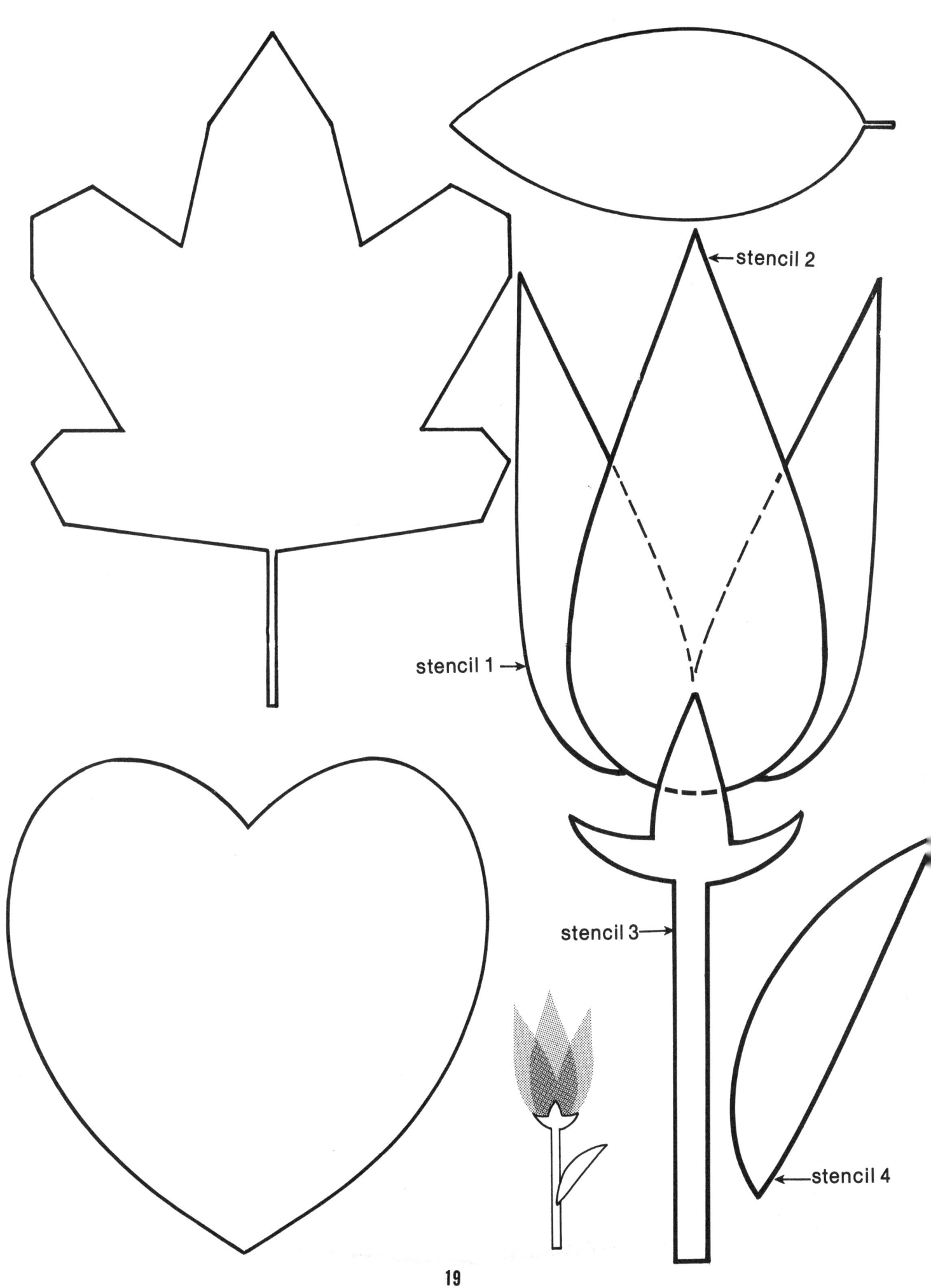

# Cut and Paste

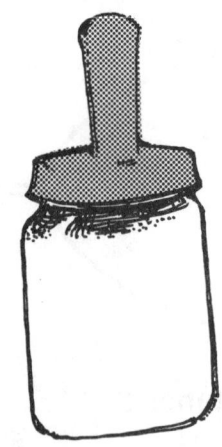
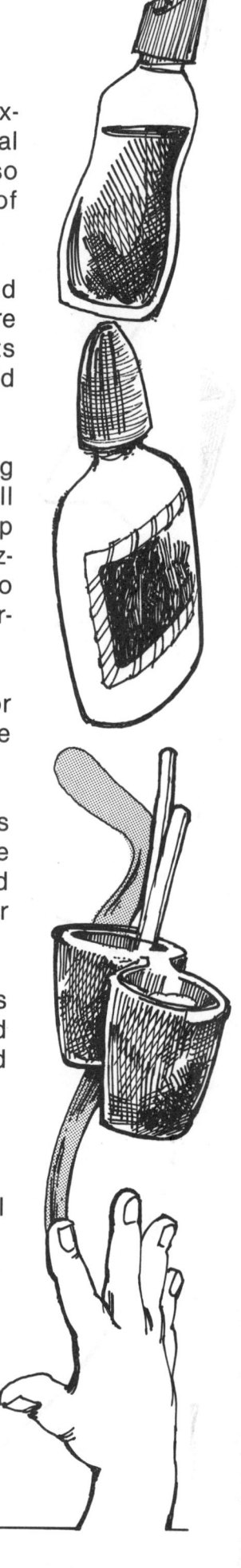

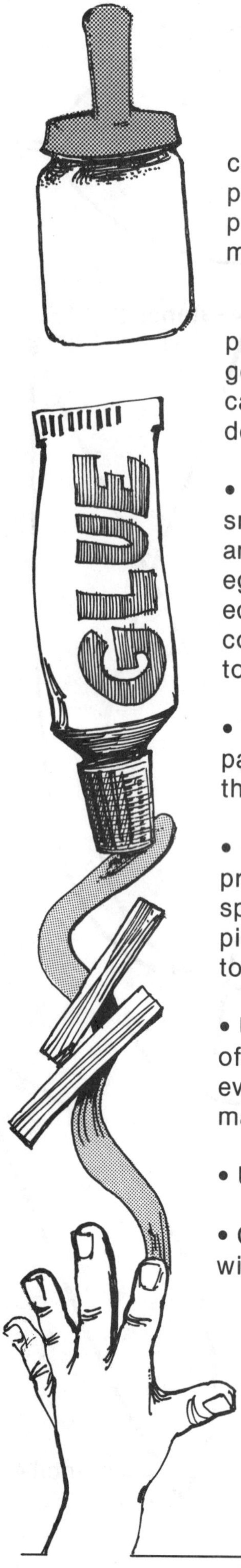

Cut and paste (or glue, whichever you prefer) can provide excellent practice in the skills of cutting, gluing (my personal preference) and listening to and following directions. It also provides opportunities for teaching the appropriate use of materials.

Because cut-and-paste activities let the children learn and practice the basic skills needed in most art projects, they are good to use in working with young children. These projects can also be VERY simple or made more difficult as the child develops.

• To help young children minimize the frustration of squeezing small amounts of glue from large glue bottles, squeeze a small amount of glue into individual containers made from cut-up egg cartons. Older children should be able to use glue squeezed directly from their bottles because they have learned how to control their squeezing motion by practicing with the egg carton sections.

• Teach the children to use only one finger when gluing or pasting. The index finger on the hand they write with is the one that seems easiest for most children to use.

• For younger children, precut the pieces using the patterns provided with the instructions. For grade school children, give specific directions and let the children cut out the needed pieces freehand. This adds originality and a unique character to each product.

• Use egg cartons cut apart to give the children small amounts of glue at a time. Ask the moms to collect them for you and even to cut them apart for you. The sections are handy and make cleanup simple.

• Use Q-tips to apply glue.

• Glue sticks can be purchased commercially and work well with young children.

20

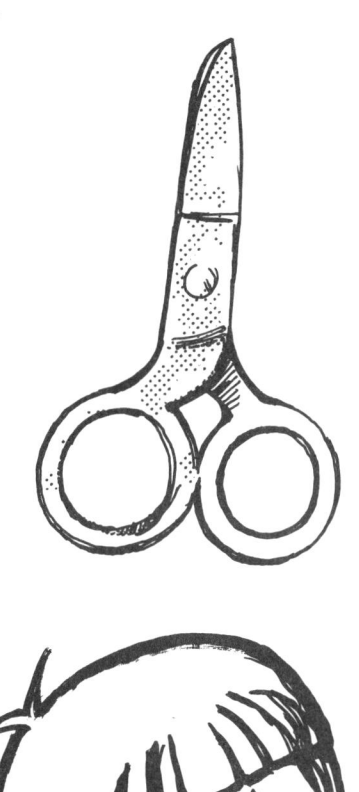

# Scissor Safety

In order to have fun using scissors, children must learn that they are a tool, not a toy. There are several activities you should discourage the children from doing while using scissors.

Don't run with scissors in your hand.

Don't put scissors in your mouth.

Don't use scissors to cut anything but paper. (This rule can be modified as children get older and use art materials like yarn, cloth or other nonpaper mediums.) Other things may be cut using scissors if you have the teacher's permission.

Don't use your scissors to poke at or point to others.

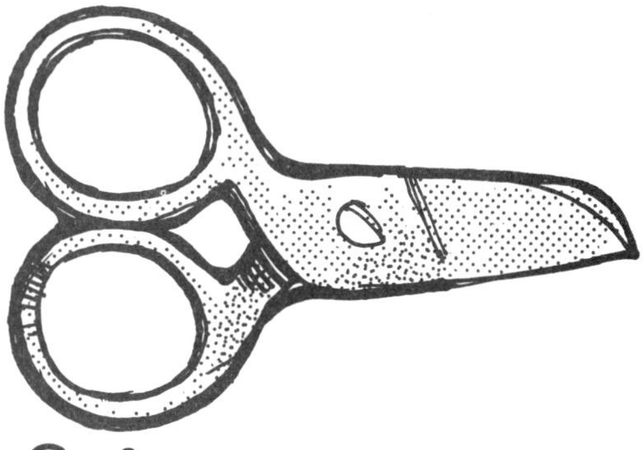

# Fun with Scissors

Using scissors can often be very frustrating for very young children. Teachers and parents should provide practice activities for the children which will sharpen their cutting skills and lessen the agony for them.

• First and most important, check each pair of scissors yourself to make sure that they open and close easily, are sharp enough to cut paper of different weights and are clean (no buildups of glue, paint or rust). Parents can check the scissors they buy before sending them to school. If they do not work properly, return them to the store and try again. This will help your child learn to use scissors with confidence and success.

• Across a piece of paper, draw lines using a heavy black marker. Start with straight lines across both the width and length of pages. The children can practice cutting using these lines. As they get better at cutting, add squiggly lines and zigzags. The following page can be reproduced for use with children. Make paper chains from the pieces! Use different colors to coordinate with the season or concept you are teaching. Several suggestions are:

**Fall**—red, yellow, and orange paper

**Halloween**—black and orange paper

**Thanksgiving**—write something you are thankful for on each strip.

**Winter**—blue and white paper

**Christmas**—red, white and green paper or write an item from your Christmas list on each strip.

**Valentine's Day**—write the name of someone you love on each strip.

**Spring**—pink, yellow and green paper

**Easter**—add lavender, purple and white paper to spring.

**Summer**—any combination of bright colors

• On large pieces of manila paper, draw LARGE shapes using a wide black marker or crayon. The children can each practice cutting around the shapes. When the shapes are cut out, let the children color in or decorate their shapes using crayons, markers or paint. Use the shapes to make class quilts, mural-sized mosaic pictures or as a background for other works of art the children have created. Try decorating the shapes first and then cutting them out. Use shapes like pumpkins, Christmas trees, hearts, Easter eggs, and kites. The stencil activity on pages 16-19 of this book can be enlarged to use with this activity also.

• Let the children cut clay or Play-Doh to strengthen their grip and improve muscle control.

• Give each of the children a 6" x 6" square of paper and let them practice snipping the paper with their scissors (small cuts that make small scraps) into a pile. Save these snips for small mosaic pictures or for confetti.

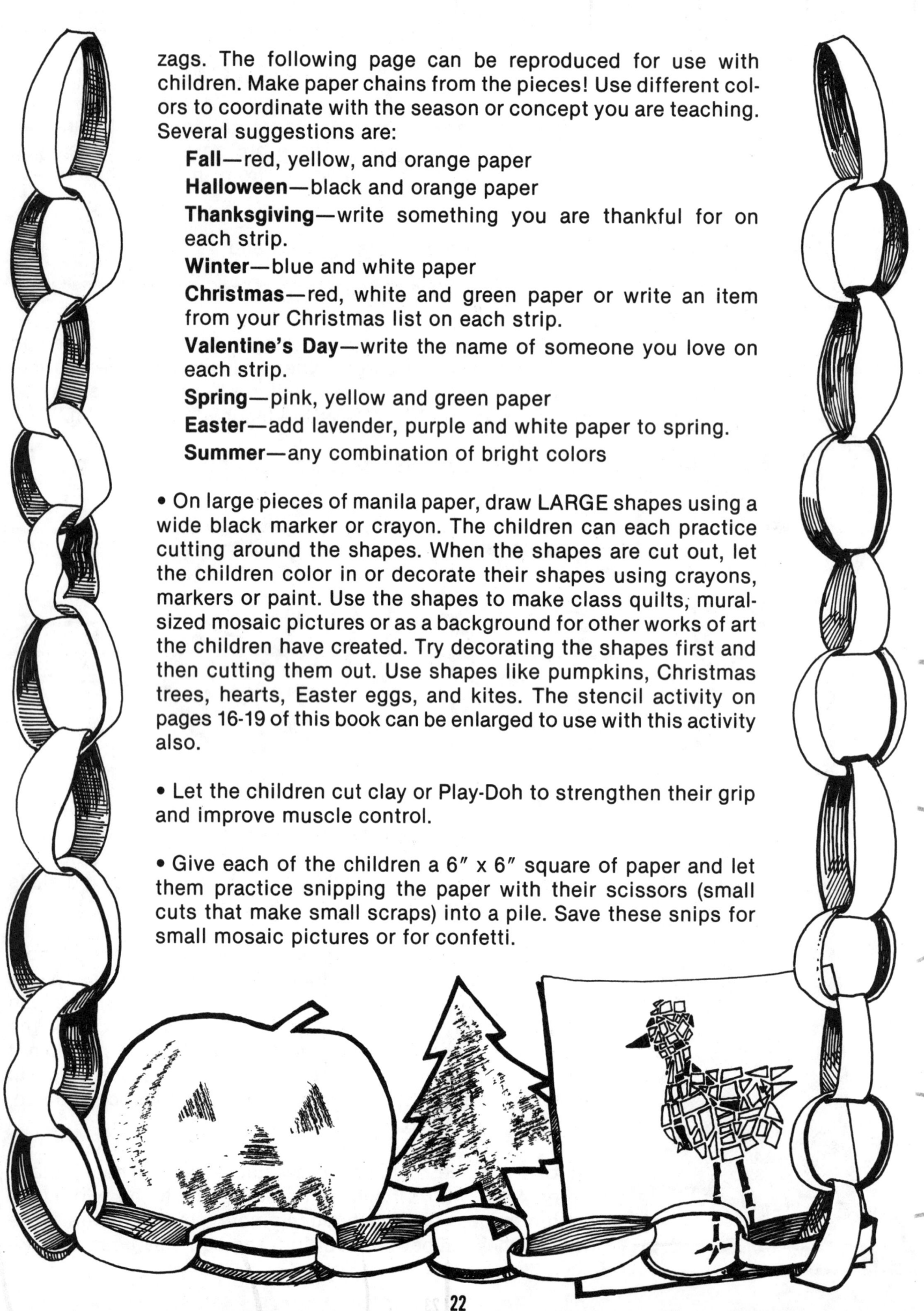

• This page may be reproduced to make pint-sized cutting practice sheets or can be drawn onto larger pieces of paper.

# Shuffling Shapes

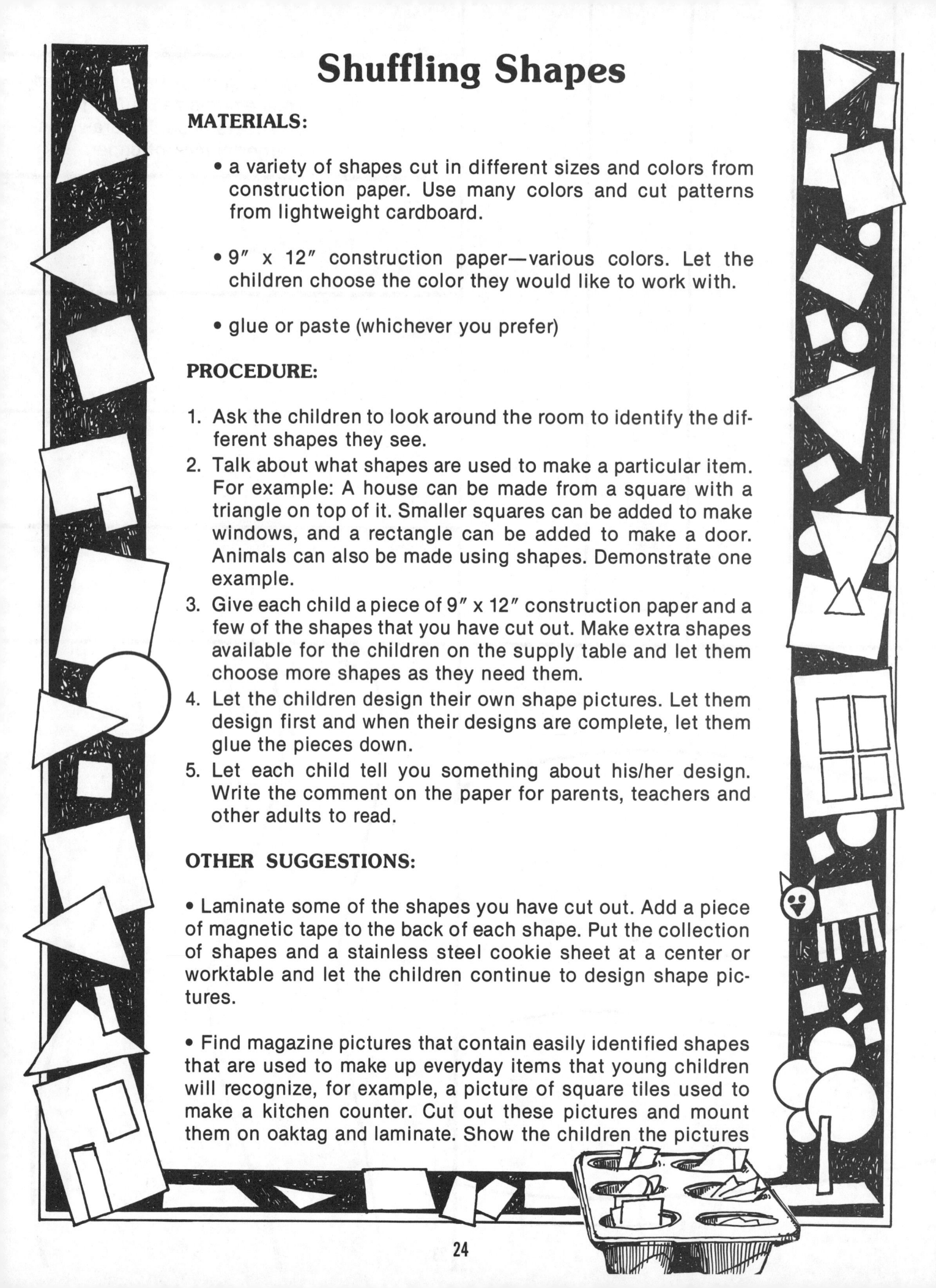

**MATERIALS:**

- a variety of shapes cut in different sizes and colors from construction paper. Use many colors and cut patterns from lightweight cardboard.

- 9" x 12" construction paper—various colors. Let the children choose the color they would like to work with.

- glue or paste (whichever you prefer)

**PROCEDURE:**

1. Ask the children to look around the room to identify the different shapes they see.
2. Talk about what shapes are used to make a particular item. For example: A house can be made from a square with a triangle on top of it. Smaller squares can be added to make windows, and a rectangle can be added to make a door. Animals can also be made using shapes. Demonstrate one example.
3. Give each child a piece of 9" x 12" construction paper and a few of the shapes that you have cut out. Make extra shapes available for the children on the supply table and let them choose more shapes as they need them.
4. Let the children design their own shape pictures. Let them design first and when their designs are complete, let them glue the pieces down.
5. Let each child tell you something about his/her design. Write the comment on the paper for parents, teachers and other adults to read.

**OTHER SUGGESTIONS:**

- Laminate some of the shapes you have cut out. Add a piece of magnetic tape to the back of each shape. Put the collection of shapes and a stainless steel cookie sheet at a center or worktable and let the children continue to design shape pictures.

- Find magazine pictures that contain easily identified shapes that are used to make up everyday items that young children will recognize, for example, a picture of square tiles used to make a kitchen counter. Cut out these pictures and mount them on oaktag and laminate. Show the children the pictures and let them identify the shapes found in each picture. The pictures could also be used in a matching center. Cut out large shapes from tagboard and laminate. Place in the center with the picture cards. Let the children match the pictures to the correct shapes.

• Older children can learn to layer their shapes and make their designs more complex. They can also experiment with 3-dimensions by bending, curling or rolling the shapes.

## Patterns for Shapes

# Apple Easy

**MATERIALS:**

- construction paper— red, brown and green
- scissors
- glue

**PROCEDURE:**

1. Reproduce the apple piece patterns and trace them onto red, green and brown construction paper.

2. Cut them out for the young children. With older children you may want to make several patterns and let them do their own tracing and cutting. Older children may also be able to cut the pieces freehand.

3. Glue the tip of the leaf to the top of the apple and the stem right next to the leaf.

4. You may also want to reproduce and trace the pattern for the white section of the apple so the children can add slices to their apples.

5. Add some dried apple seeds to the white sections for a more authentic look. About a week before doing this project, ask the children's moms to start saving apple seeds to send to school.

• Use yellow, green or dark red paper to make the different varieties of apples. Bring in samples of each variety and when the craft project is done, have a tasting party.

• Put a large tree trunk made of construction paper on your door or bulletin board; add lots of leaves to it and use it to display your delicious looking apples when they are finished.

# Sassy Cats

**MATERIALS:**

- construction paper—black, pink and green
- glue (squeezed into egg cartons cut apart)
- white crayons or chalk

**PROCEDURE:**

1. Reproduce the face, eye, ear and nose patterns. Cut them out and trace onto oaktag. Trace enough patterns for each child in your class.

2. Cut out the pieces for younger children. Older children can trace and cut out the patterns for themselves. They may also be able to cut the needed pieces out freehand.

3. Each child will glue the eyes and nose onto the face of the cat. Pupils can be added by using a black crayon or marker or a bit of black scrap paper.

4. Each child will glue the wide end of the ears onto the back of the face. Scraps of pink paper can be added to the middle of the ears.

5. Have each child draw whiskers and a mouth on the face of the cat, using a white crayon.

Cat's Face—Cut 1

**OTHER SUGGESTIONS:**

• This pattern can also be used to make cats of different "catty" colors. Lions and tigers can also be made by adding manes of yarn or some black strips.

• Use spaghetti noodles or kite string to make the whiskers.

• Precut pieces of yarn about 2" long to make a more furry cat. Dip the ends of the yarn in glue and place them on the front of the cat.

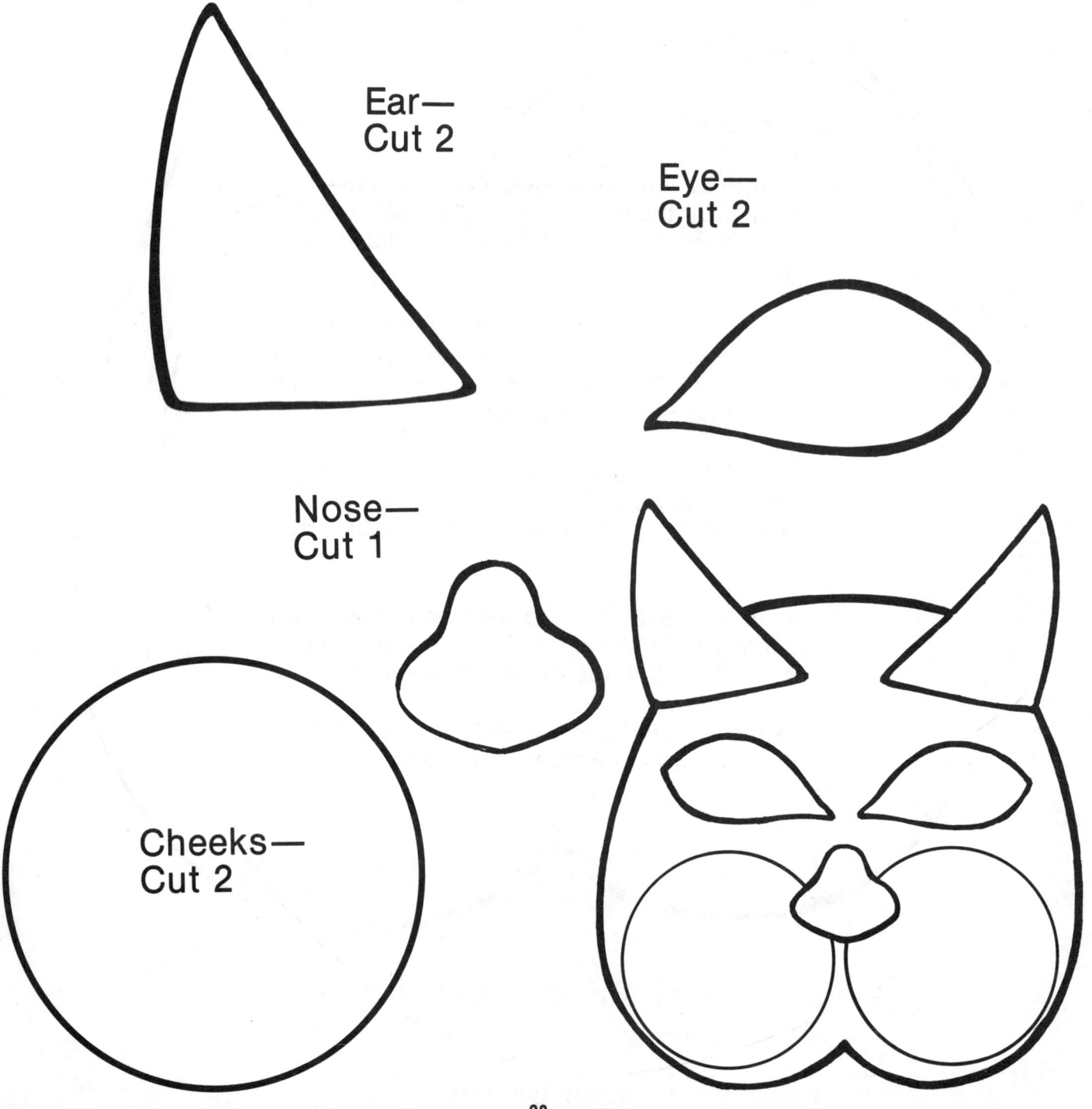

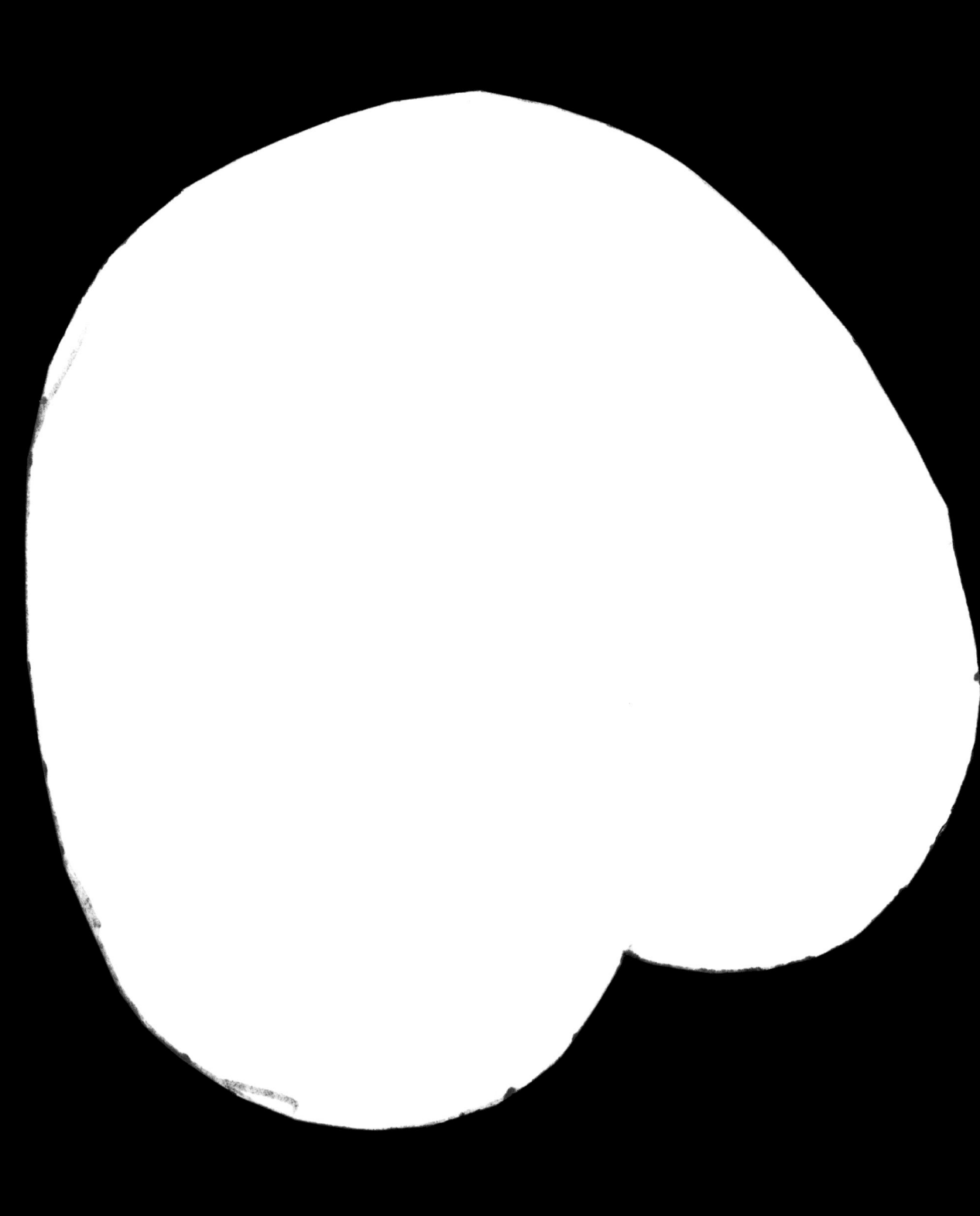

# Fanciful Flock

**MATERIALS:**

- construction paper—black, blue or red (or any other color you would like to make your birds. You might also like to provide a variety of different colors and let the children choose the color of bird they would like to make) for the bird's head, body, wings and tail.

- construction paper—yellow or orange for the beak and feet and white or black for the eyes.

- scissors

- glue (squeezed into egg cartons cut apart)

**PROCEDURE:**

1. Cut the main color (head and body) into strips as follows:
   - body—3" x 12"
   - head—3" x 6"
2. Reproduce the patterns for the wings, tail, beak, and feet. Trace them onto oaktag. Cut them out. Trace the pieces on construction paper so each child will have one set. Cut them out. Older children may trace and cut out their own or try their luck at freehand cutting.
3. Give each child the needed pieces.
4. Glue the ends of each strip together to make a loop. Remind the children to pinch the ends together tightly and count to 10. By this time the loops should be secure.
5. Glue the two loops together to look like a figure 8. These loops will be the bird's head and body.
6. Each child will glue the flat edges of the wings to the sides of the body just below the head.
7. Glue the flat edge of the tail to the bottom of the large loop.
8. Fold the beak in half and glue to the top of the small loop. The beak should point away from the tail, not in the same direction.
9. Glue the flat edge of the feet to the bottom of the large loop. The feet should point the same way the beak does.

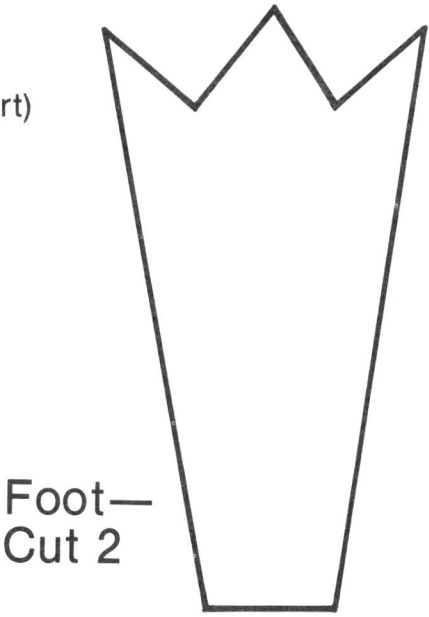

Foot— Cut 2

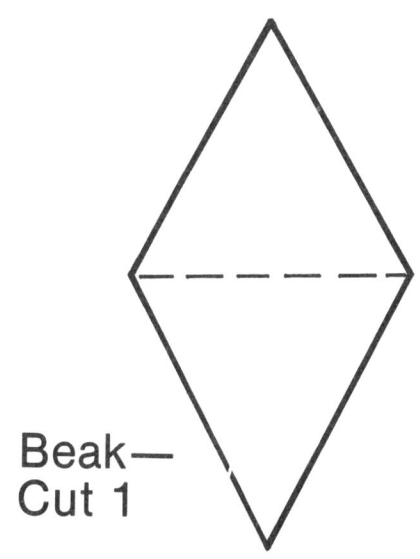

Beak— Cut 1

29

**OTHER SUGGESTIONS:**

• Attach a piece of string to each bird's head and hang the birds from the ceiling, or string a wire across the room and the birds can roost on your "telephone wire."

• Older kids can research the songbird or state bird of their choice and do the construction as an independent activity. The birds can then be displayed with a collection of nests, pictures, reports, and drawings.

Tail—Cut 1

Wing—Cut 2

# Feathery Friends

**MATERIALS:**

- fluff feathers (These are sold in most craft stores.)
- 9" × 12" construction paper—assorted colors
- scissors
- markers
- pictures of Indian costumes

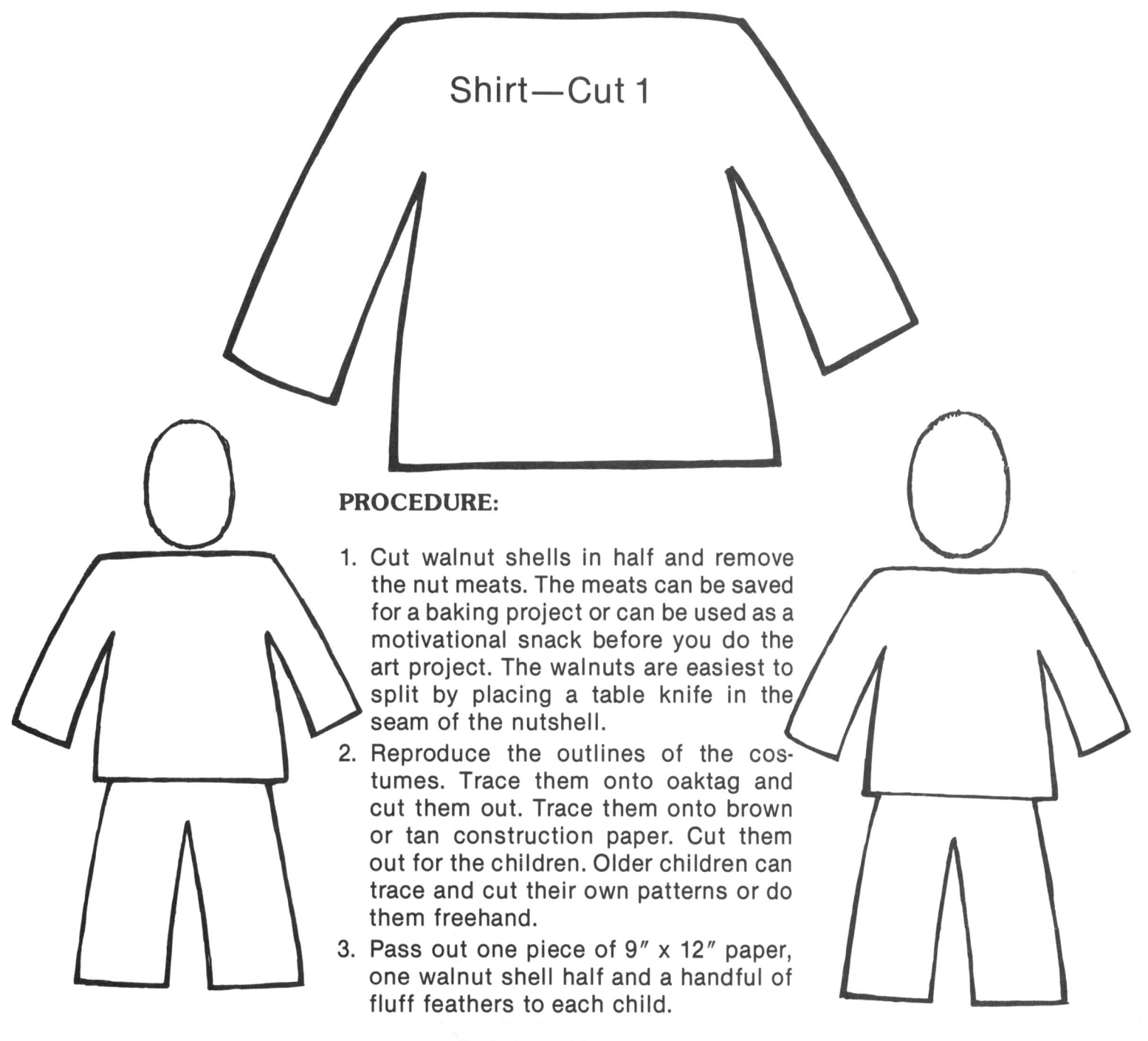

Shirt—Cut 1

**PROCEDURE:**

1. Cut walnut shells in half and remove the nut meats. The meats can be saved for a baking project or can be used as a motivational snack before you do the art project. The walnuts are easiest to split by placing a table knife in the seam of the nutshell.
2. Reproduce the outlines of the costumes. Trace them onto oaktag and cut them out. Trace them onto brown or tan construction paper. Cut them out for the children. Older children can trace and cut their own patterns or do them freehand.
3. Pass out one piece of 9" × 12" paper, one walnut shell half and a handful of fluff feathers to each child.

Pants—Cut 1

Each child will put glue around the edge of the walnut shell and press it to the paper about 1/3 of the way from the top.

5. Then the child will glue the feathers to the paper around the top of the walnut shell. Have extra feathers available for those children who want to make a fuller headdress.

6. While the feathers are drying, talk about the types of clothes Indians have worn traditionally. Discuss the kinds of decorations you might have found on their clothing. Show the children several pictures of traditional Indian dress.

7. Each child will glue the shirt and pants to the 9" x 12" paper just below the face and headdress.

8. When the glue on the clothes has dried, let the children use markers and scraps of paper to decorate the clothing. Yarn may be used for hair.

**OTHER SUGGESTIONS:**

• Use different types of seeds to decorate the clothes.

• Let the children make Indian vests from grocery sacks and decorate them like the clothing on their Indians.

• Divide older children into groups and assign each group a different tribe, for example, Navajo, Crow, Sioux or Seminole. Let the children research the traditional tribal dress of their tribe. Have them complete the craft project. When the costumes are finished, let each group make a class presentation telling about and showing the costumes they have made.

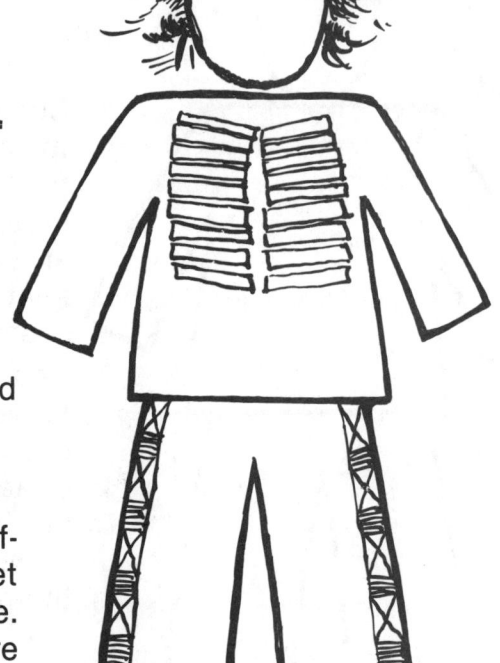

# "Up-Standing" Turkeys

**MATERIALS:**

- dinner-sized paper plates
- construction paper—assorted colors
- glue
- scissors
- crayons, markers

**PROCEDURE:**

1. Reproduce the patterns provided and trace them onto oaktag. Cut them out and trace the feather pattern onto various colors of construction paper. You will need at least ten feathers for each child. Trace the head pattern onto folded brown construction paper.
2. Cut out the pieces. Older children may trace and cut out the pieces themselves or may try to cut them freehand.
3. Pass out one set of pieces to each child.
4. Pass out 1 paper plate to each child. Using crayons or markers, color the inside circle on both sides of the plate. Color the rippled part with bright colors for feathers.
5. After the coloring is done, turn the plate upside down and fold the bottom one-third of the plate up toward you and crease it so it will stay.
6. With the flat edge of the plate on the bottom, fold the paper plate in half to form a V. This V should allow the plate to stand upright without support.
7. Pass out 10 feathers to each child. Let the children fringe the rounded edges and sides of the feathers.
8. Glue these feathers around the outside edge of the paper plate where the brightly colored ripples are.
9. Give 1 turkey head to each child. Each child will decorate the head and glue it to the fold at the front of the paper plate.

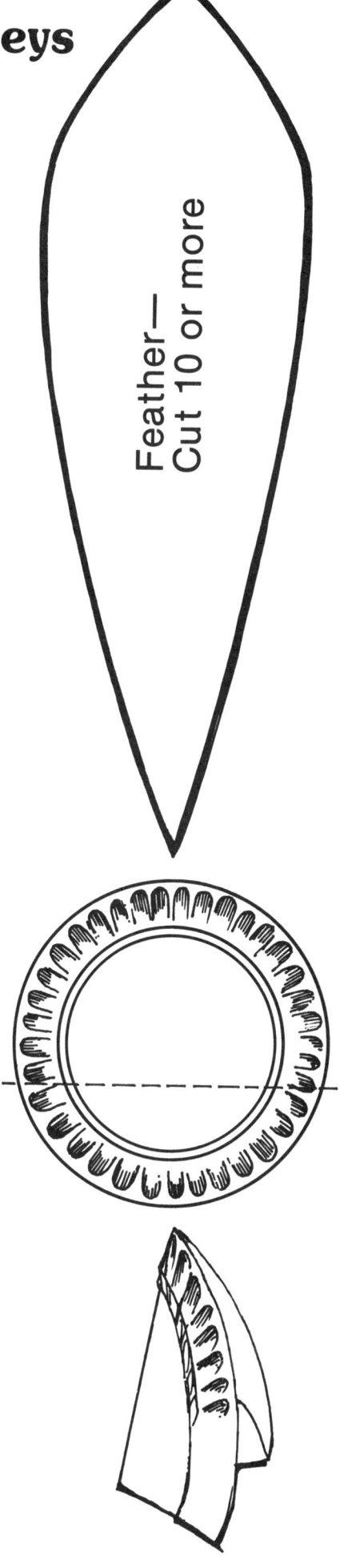

Feather—Cut 10 or more

33

**OTHER SUGGESTIONS:**

• You can also use the fluff feathers instead of multicolored construction paper to make a more interesting tail.

• Set the turkeys on shelves, desks or tables for decoration. These turkeys also make neat centerpieces for the children to take home for their Thanksgiving tables.

• Small turkeys can be made from dessert-sized paper plates and used as place cards.

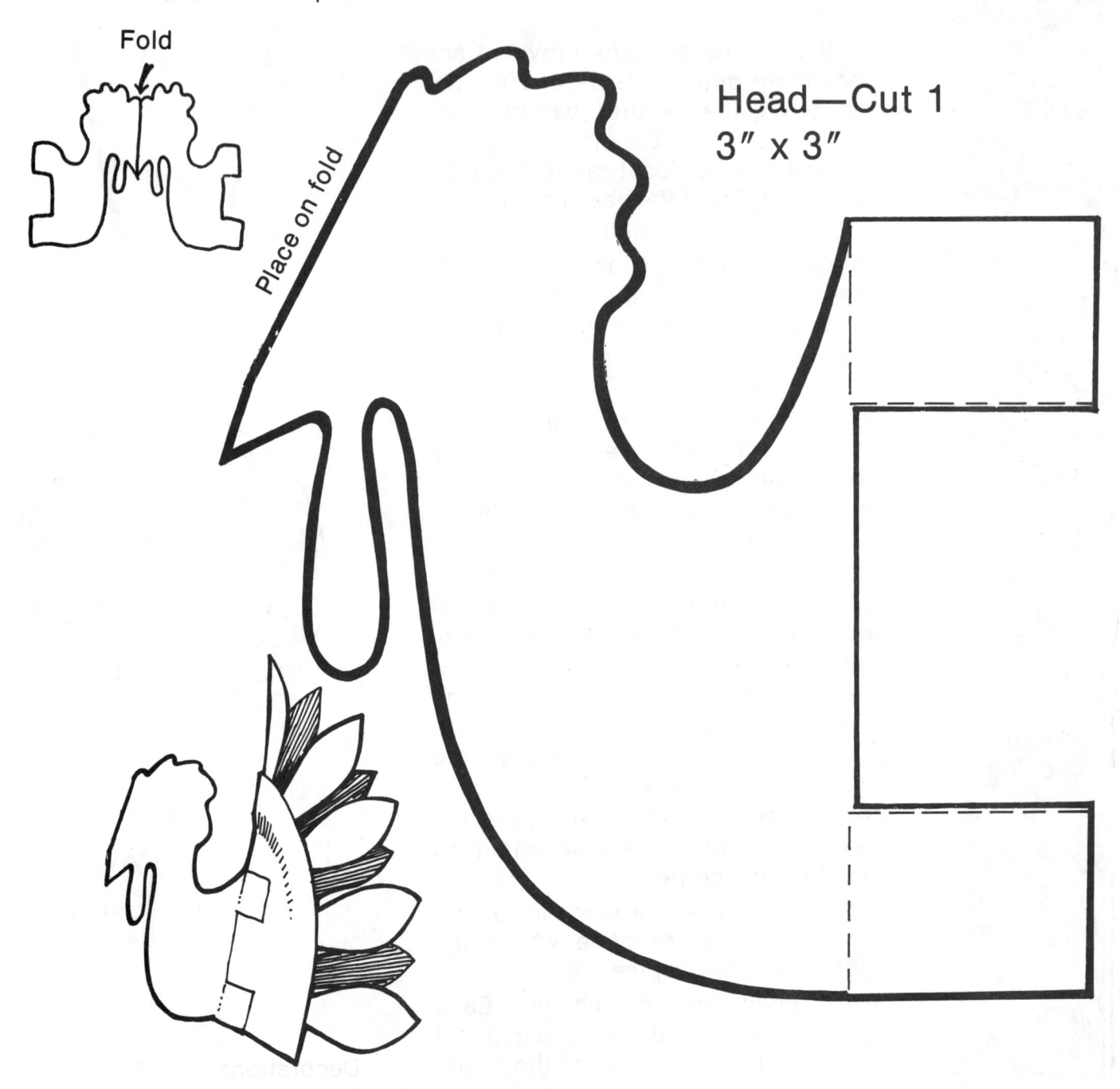

Fold

Place on fold

Head—Cut 1
3" x 3"

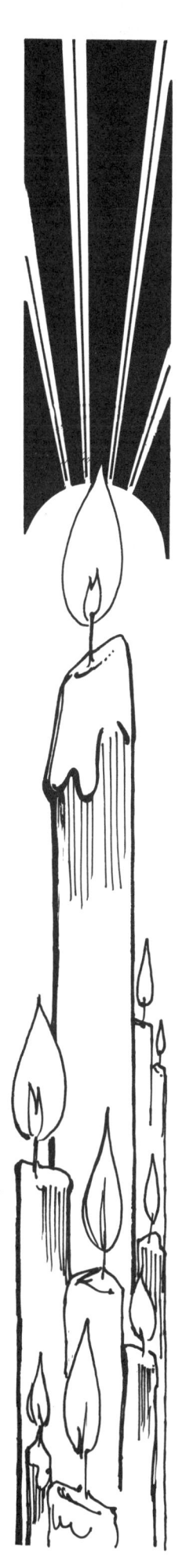

# Brightly Shining T.P. Rolls

**MATERIALS:**

- empty toilet paper rolls—ask children's moms to save them
- construction paper—a variety of bright colors
- glue
- scissors
- construction paper scraps

**PROCEDURE:**

1. Cut the construction paper into rectangles that will cover the toilet paper roll.

2. Reproduce and trace the flame pattern onto oaktag and cut it out. Trace one flame for each child onto yellow construction paper with the top of the flame on the fold. Cut the flames out. Older children can trace and cut out their own flames or cut them freehand.

3. Pass out one toilet paper roll to each child. Pass out one piece of construction paper to cover the roll.

4. Each child will then cover the toilet paper roll. Put glue on the PAPER, NOT ON THE ROLL. Glue around the edges and drizzle glue along the center. Lay the roll down on the glued paper and begin to roll until the roll is covered.

5. Glue the rounded edges of the flame to opposite sides inside the roll.

6. Let each child decorate his "candle" the way he would like, using paper scraps and glue. Seasonal themes for Hanukkah and Christmas can be used, or the children can choose designs of their own.

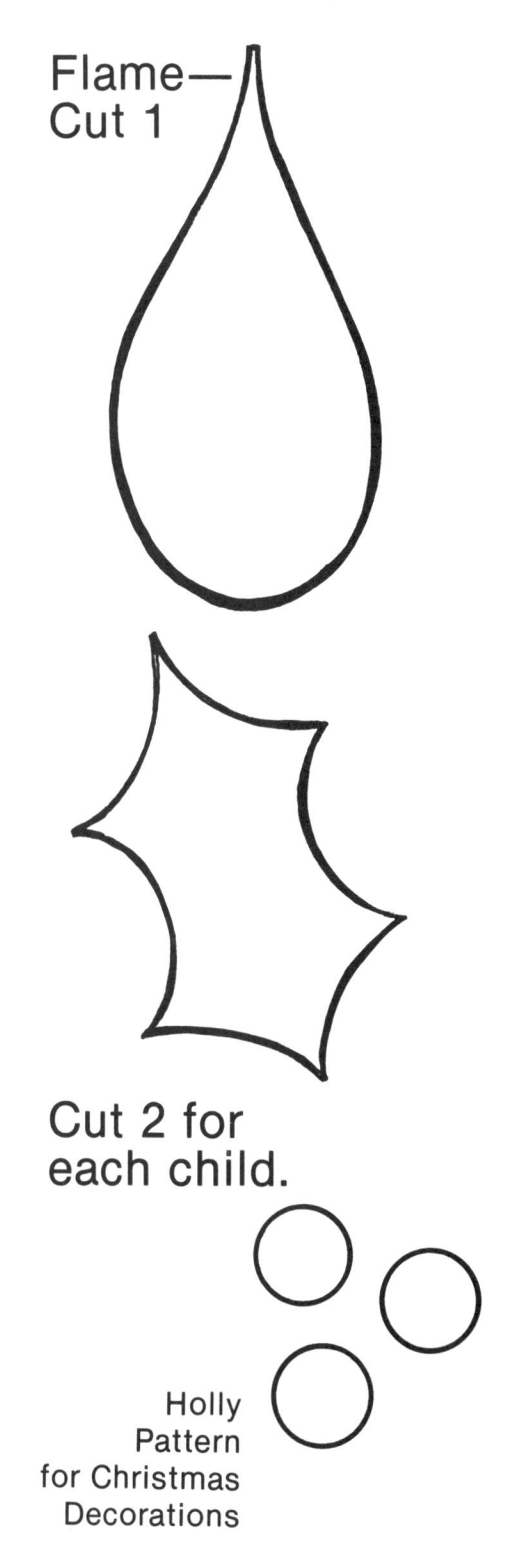

Flame—Cut 1

Cut 2 for each child.

Holly Pattern for Christmas Decorations

**OTHER SUGGESTIONS:**

• These candles make a nice bulletin board display or can be used as centerpieces and surrounded by evergreen garland.

• Use paper towel rolls or the rolls from gift wrap to make taller candles of different widths.

• Use foil Christmas paper instead of construction paper to cover the rolls being used.

• Use brightly colored paper to make birthday candles according to the directions. On each child's candle write the child's name and birth date. Let each child cut out a picture of what he would like for his birthday. Use old magazines or catalogues to find pictures. Each child will glue the picture to his candle. To display the children's birthdays, make a large birthday cake on the bulletin board. Attach the candles to the cake top with thumbtacks. As you celebrate each birthday, take down the child's candle so he can take it home.

# Snowman Mobiles

**MATERIALS:**

- construction paper—white, brown and assorted colors
- string or yarn
- glue
- scissors
- crayons or markers

**PROCEDURE:**

1. Reproduce the patterns of the hat, scarf, twig and circles. Trace them onto oaktag and cut them out.
2. Trace the patterns onto construction paper and cut out the pieces for the children to use. Older children can trace and cut out their own patterns or cut them freehand.
3. Give each child one set of pieces and one length of string.
4. Each child will attach the 5" circles to the string by laying one circle on the table and dotting it with glue around the edges and in the center of it. Lay the end of the string across the circle that has been dotted with glue. Place the second circle over the top and press all three layers together.
5. Repeat steps 1 and 2 to attach the 4" circles.
6. Glue the single end of the twig pieces to the 4" circle.
7. Let the child fringe one end of the scarf piece. Glue the scarf just above the 4" circle on the string.
8. Attach the 3" circle above the scarf using the same method as before.
9. Attach the hat to the top of the snowman.

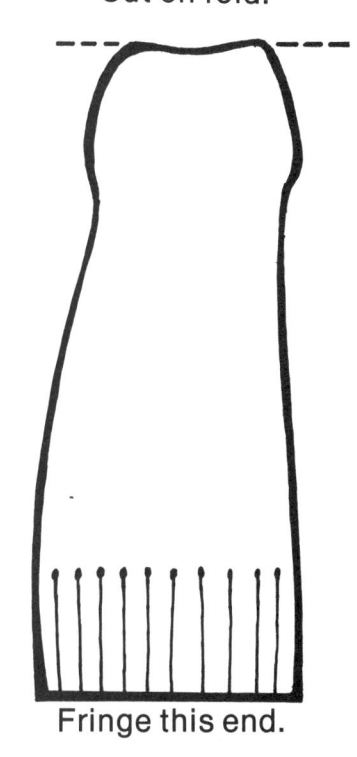

Hat—Cut 2

Cut on fold.

Fringe this end.

Scarf—Cut 2

10. Hang the children's snowmen from the ceiling or a clothesline for a frosty winter feeling.

**OTHER SUGGESTIONS:**

• Use scraps of cloth and yarn for the hat and scarf.

• Dab white paint onto blue paper with small pieces of sponge. Let the paint dry. Trace the circle patterns onto this paper and finish the snowmen as directed.

• Staple around the edges of the pieces of the snowman leaving a small opening on one side. Stuff each piece with small amounts of crumpled newspaper. Staple the openings shut. Staple small pieces of string between the sections.

Twig (Arm)—Cut 2

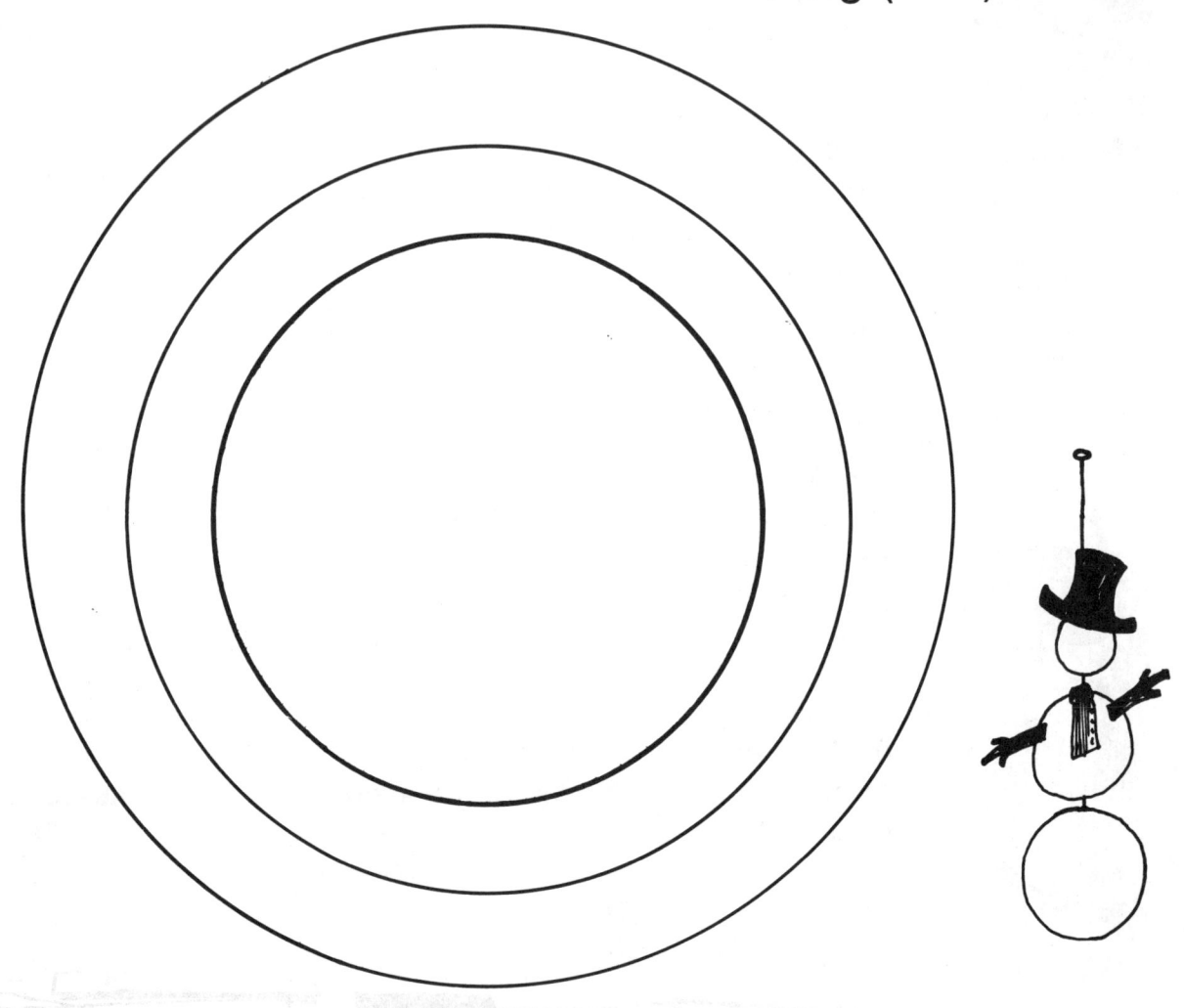

# Fluttering Flags

**MATERIALS:**

- 9" x 12" construction paper—red, white and blue
- scissors
- glue
- star stickers

**PROCEDURE:**

1. Reproduce the pattern on the following page. Cut out and trace onto oaktag. Cut out the oaktag pattern. Trace the square onto blue paper. Cut out seven ½" x 12" red stripes and one blue square for each child. Older children can trace and cut out their own pieces.

2. Give each child one 9" x 12" piece of white construction paper, seven red stripes and one blue square.

3. Each child will glue one red stripe across the top of the white paper and one red stripe across the bottom of the white paper.

4. Let each child lay his remaining five strips of paper in place across the flag. When the child is happy with the way he has arranged the stripes, he may glue them to the white paper.

5. After the stripes have been glued down, each child will glue the blue square to the upper left-hand corner of the striped paper.

6. Give each child several gummed stars to place on the blue square.

Stripe Pattern—Cut 7

**OTHER SUGGESTIONS:**

• Let the children use white crayons to draw their own stars or provide star stencils (see page 17 for pattern) to decorate their fields of blue.

• Let the children make flags from different periods of American history. Show them several examples of American flags. Change the arrangement of the stars for something a little different.

• Make your state flag.

• Let the children design and make flags for their own country. The flag should tell others a little bit about the person who made it.

• Make the flags and visit a local Veteran's hospital. Present the flags to those veterans that rarely receive company or gifts. Check with the Public Relations Office at the hospital for more details.

Square Pattern—
Cut 1

# Lovely Lambs

**MATERIALS:**

- paper plates
- construction paper—white and purple
- crayons or markers

**PROCEDURE:**

1. Cut the white paper into 10" circles and the purple paper into 11" circles.

2. Reproduce the patterns for the eyes, nose and ears of the lamb. Cut them out and trace onto oaktag. Cut out these patterns and use them to trace the pieces onto construction paper. Cut out enough pieces for each child.

3. Pass out 1 paper plate to each child.

4. Each child will glue the eyes and nose to the center of the paper plate.

5. Each child will glue the pointed ends of the ears to the back of the paper plate.

6. Pass out 1 purple and 1 white circle to each child. Let the children fringe the edges of each circle.

7. Glue the white circle on top of the purple circle.

8. Put dots of glue around the outside edge of the paper plate. Glue the plate to the fringed circles. Your lamb is now ready to help you celebrate spring!

**OTHER SUGGESTIONS:**

- Use yarn to make loops of "wool" around the edge of the plate instead of using the paper circles. You could also use scraps of fleece material.

- Visit a sheep farm. Let the children see lambs, sheep shearing and the spinning of wool. If possible bring back enough of the clean wool to glue around the edges of their paper plates.

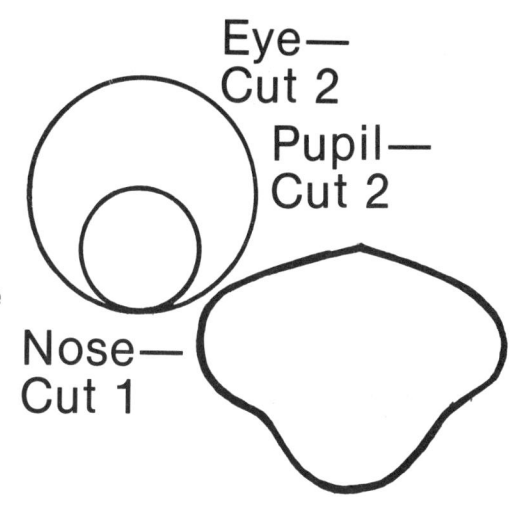

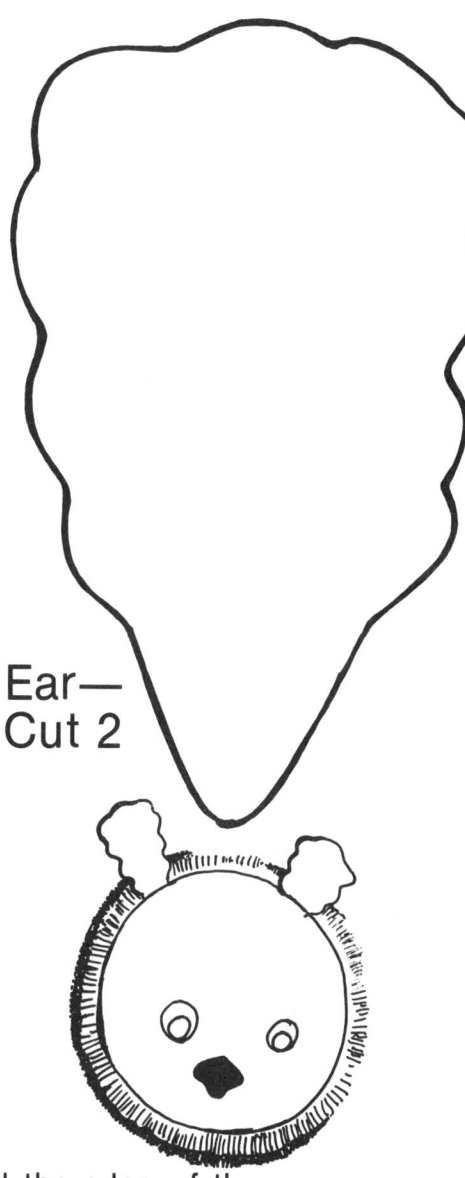

# Loop Flowers

**MATERIALS:**

- 12" x 18" construction paper—assorted colors
- glue
- scissors

**PROCEDURE:**

1. Cut the 12" x 18" construction paper into 2" x 18" strips. Use colors like yellow, red, orange, pink, blue, purple, etc. Cut 5 to 8 strips per child. Also cut 1 green 12" x 18" strip per child.

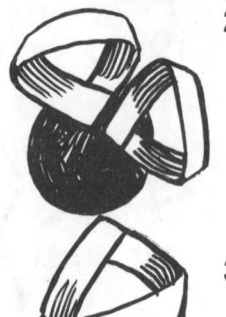

2. Reproduce the patterns provided and trace them onto oaktag. Cut them out and trace the leaves onto green paper and the circles onto black, brown, dark blue or yellow. Older children can trace and cut their own pieces.

3. Give each child 1 stem, 2 leaves and 2 center circles.

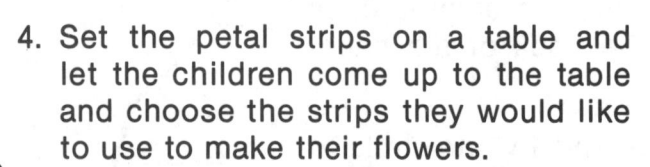

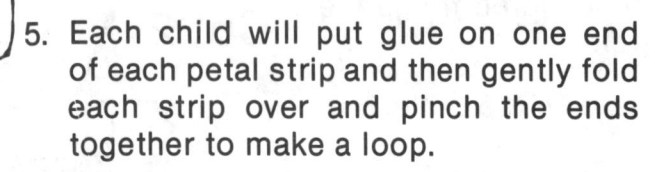

4. Set the petal strips on a table and let the children come up to the table and choose the strips they would like to use to make their flowers.

5. Each child will put glue on one end of each petal strip and then gently fold each strip over and pinch the ends together to make a loop.

6. After the loops have been made, glue the straight end of each petal near the outside edge of the center circle.

7. Glue one end of the stem near the edge of the center circle.

8. Glue the remaining center over the petal and stem ends. This will hold the petals on a little better and will make them stand out.

9. Glue the rounded ends of the leaves to the stem.

42

**OTHER SUGGESTIONS:**

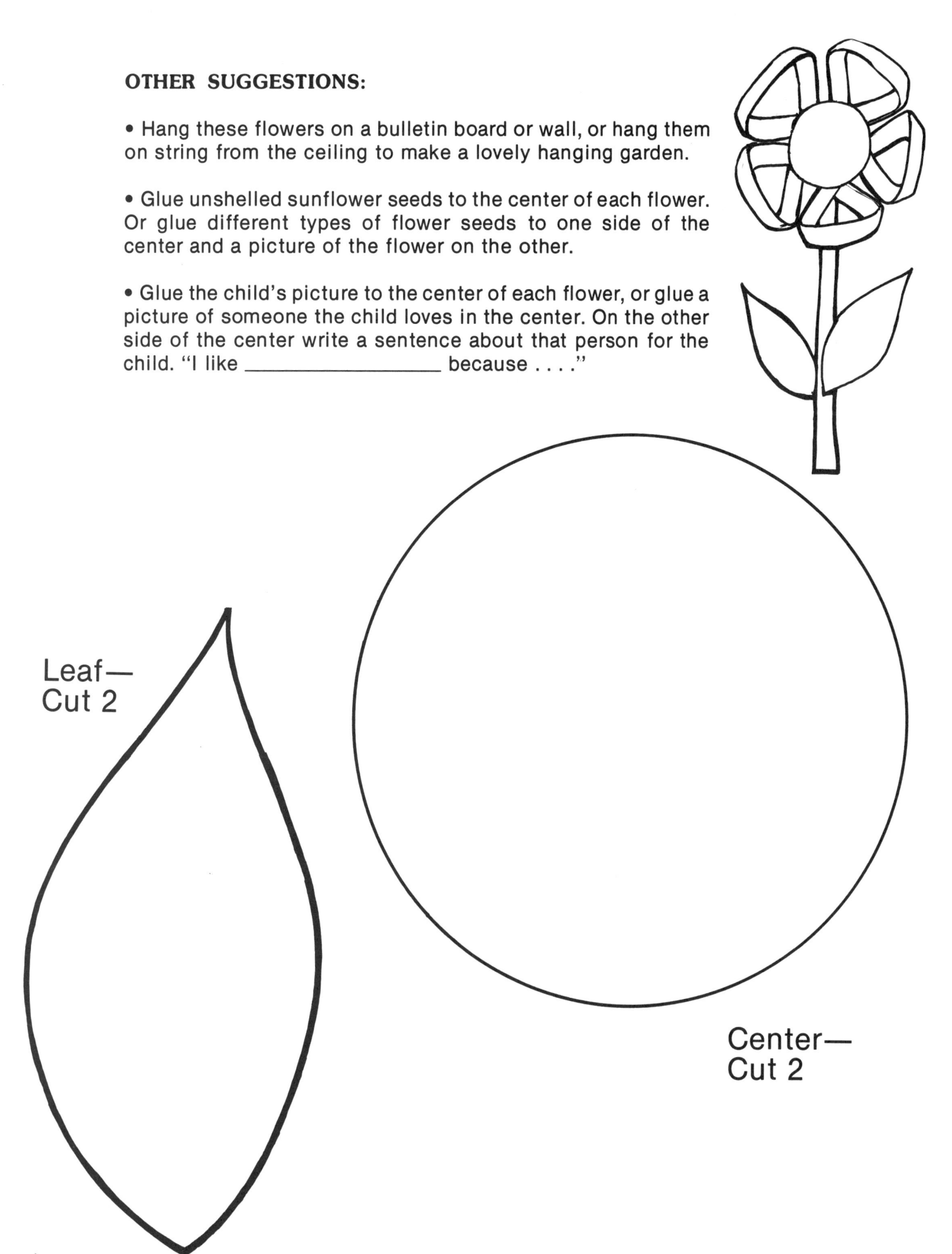

• Hang these flowers on a bulletin board or wall, or hang them on string from the ceiling to make a lovely hanging garden.

• Glue unshelled sunflower seeds to the center of each flower. Or glue different types of flower seeds to one side of the center and a picture of the flower on the other.

• Glue the child's picture to the center of each flower, or glue a picture of someone the child loves in the center. On the other side of the center write a sentence about that person for the child. "I like _____ because . . . ."

Leaf—
Cut 2

Center—
Cut 2

# Painting

Painting can be a very exciting, pleasant activity or it can be a horrifying experience for both teacher and children. It takes planning on the part of the teacher or parent. Some things to take into consideration when planning a painting activity are:

- the type of paint you will use and how you will distribute it. You can use egg cartons once for distributing tempera paint. Styrofoam meat trays also work well, and parents can easily collect these items.

- the seating arrangement of your class for the project.

- covering desks or tabletops; wearing paint shirts, etc.

- where you will hang or dry the completed paintings—wooden or plastic clothes drying racks are great when used with pinch clothespins. Clotheslines strung across a corner of a room work great, too.

- cleanup procedures—for quick cleanup, set a bucket of warm soapy water on an empty worktable. Set paper towels on the table, too. Set the wastebasket on the floor next to the table. As the children finish painting, they can quietly come up to the table to wash their hands. When each child is finished, direct him to an area where you have other activities prepared.

Painting can give children freedom of movement, a sense of color and many other valuable experiences. Teachers should provide children with different types of paint, different types and sizes of paintbrushes and other painting tools like string, sponges and straws. Children should also be given the opportunity to use their hands and other parts of their bodies (feet, tongues for pudding painting, etc.) to paint. Teachers should also provide a wide variety of colors to mix and match.

Here is a good paint recipe that the children will enjoy mixing.

**FINGER PAINT**
   1 envelope unflavored gelatin
   cold water
   1/2 c. cornstarch
   4 tbsp. dishwashing liquid
   food coloring

Stir gelatin into 1/3 c. cold water; set aside. Put cornstarch and 2 1/2 c. cold water into saucepan and stir until dissolved. Bring mixture to a simmer and stir constantly until thickened. Remove from heat and blend in gelatin and dishwashing liquid. Let cool slightly. Put 1/2 c. mixture into container for each color. Cool completely. Cover and store at room temperature.

# Other Ways to Use Paint

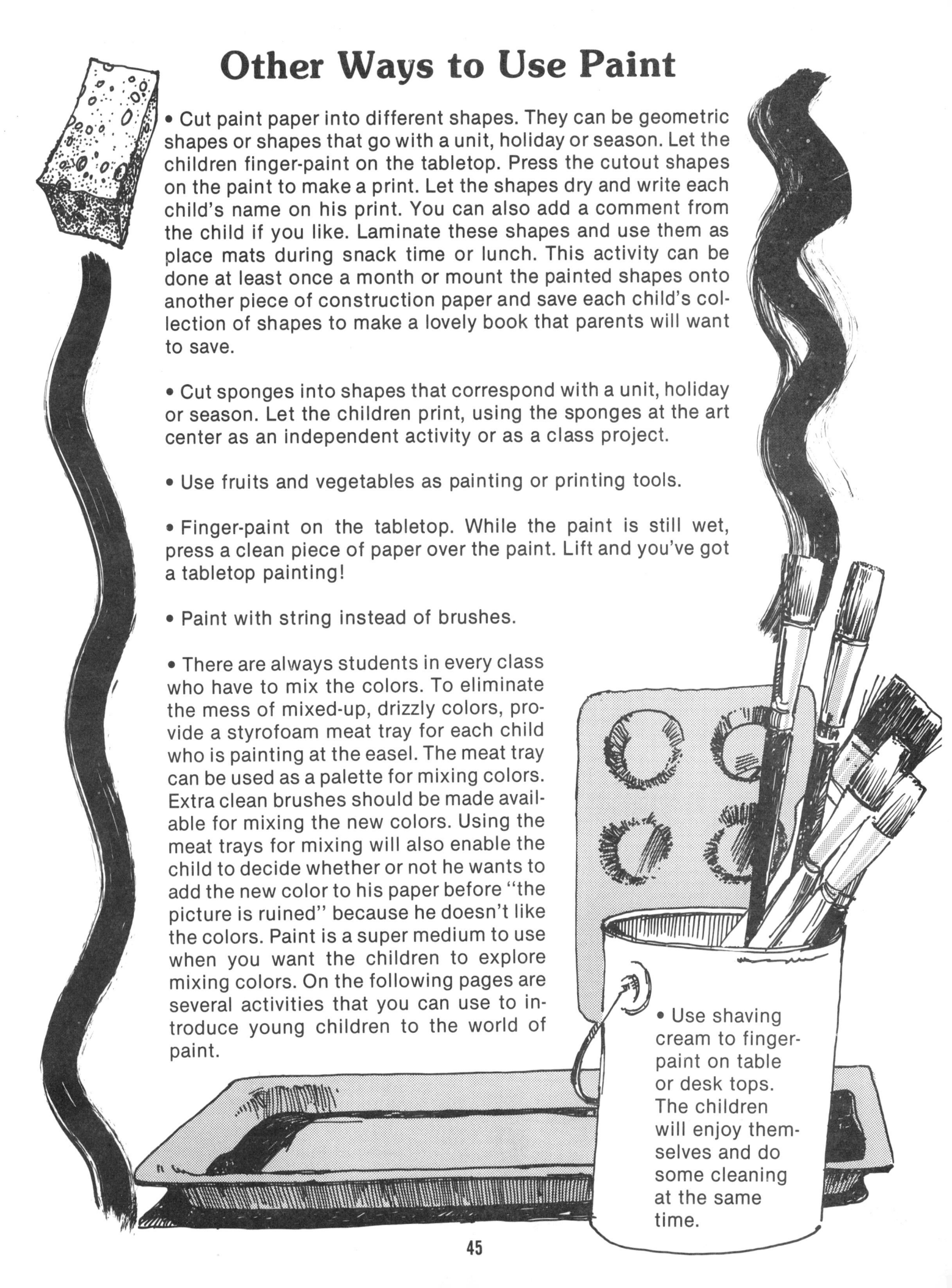

• Cut paint paper into different shapes. They can be geometric shapes or shapes that go with a unit, holiday or season. Let the children finger-paint on the tabletop. Press the cutout shapes on the paint to make a print. Let the shapes dry and write each child's name on his print. You can also add a comment from the child if you like. Laminate these shapes and use them as place mats during snack time or lunch. This activity can be done at least once a month or mount the painted shapes onto another piece of construction paper and save each child's collection of shapes to make a lovely book that parents will want to save.

• Cut sponges into shapes that correspond with a unit, holiday or season. Let the children print, using the sponges at the art center as an independent activity or as a class project.

• Use fruits and vegetables as painting or printing tools.

• Finger-paint on the tabletop. While the paint is still wet, press a clean piece of paper over the paint. Lift and you've got a tabletop painting!

• Paint with string instead of brushes.

• There are always students in every class who have to mix the colors. To eliminate the mess of mixed-up, drizzly colors, provide a styrofoam meat tray for each child who is painting at the easel. The meat tray can be used as a palette for mixing colors. Extra clean brushes should be made available for mixing the new colors. Using the meat trays for mixing will also enable the child to decide whether or not he wants to add the new color to his paper before "the picture is ruined" because he doesn't like the colors. Paint is a super medium to use when you want the children to explore mixing colors. On the following pages are several activities that you can use to introduce young children to the world of paint.

• Use shaving cream to finger-paint on table or desk tops. The children will enjoy themselves and do some cleaning at the same time.

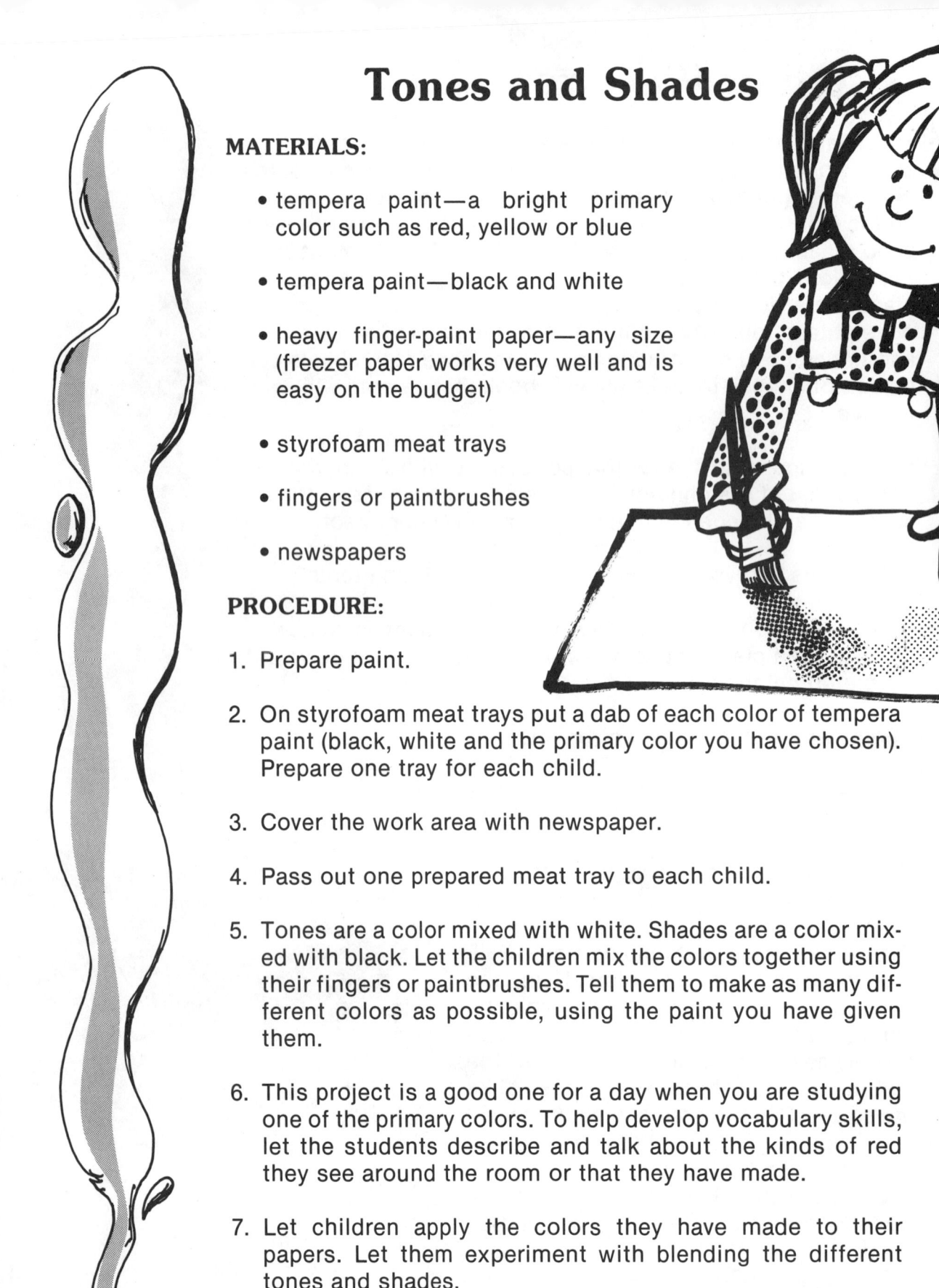

# Tones and Shades

**MATERIALS:**

- tempera paint—a bright primary color such as red, yellow or blue

- tempera paint—black and white

- heavy finger-paint paper—any size (freezer paper works very well and is easy on the budget)

- styrofoam meat trays

- fingers or paintbrushes

- newspapers

**PROCEDURE:**

1. Prepare paint.

2. On styrofoam meat trays put a dab of each color of tempera paint (black, white and the primary color you have chosen). Prepare one tray for each child.

3. Cover the work area with newspaper.

4. Pass out one prepared meat tray to each child.

5. Tones are a color mixed with white. Shades are a color mixed with black. Let the children mix the colors together using their fingers or paintbrushes. Tell them to make as many different colors as possible, using the paint you have given them.

6. This project is a good one for a day when you are studying one of the primary colors. To help develop vocabulary skills, let the students describe and talk about the kinds of red they see around the room or that they have made.

7. Let children apply the colors they have made to their papers. Let them experiment with blending the different tones and shades.

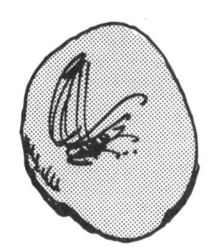

8. When they are finished, hang the painting to dry.

9. After the paintings have dried, let each child tell you something about his painting. Write the comment on the paper and invite parents to come in and learn about colors from their children.

**OTHER SUGGESTIONS:**

• Another variation of this project can be done by giving each child a dab of each primary color (red, yellow and blue) with the black and white paint, also. By adding the three primary colors instead of just one, the children now have the freedom to make new colors as well as tones and shades. Remember the styrofoam meat trays make excellent palettes.

• Let the children finger-paint the tones and shades they have made on the tabletop. Press a piece of paper over the painted design to make a print.

• Use a contrasting color of construction paper to paint on or make a print with.

• Add brown paint to the palette instead of black. What happens to the colors then? How is it different from mixing with black?

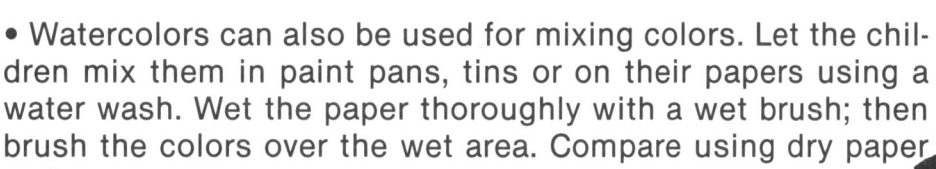

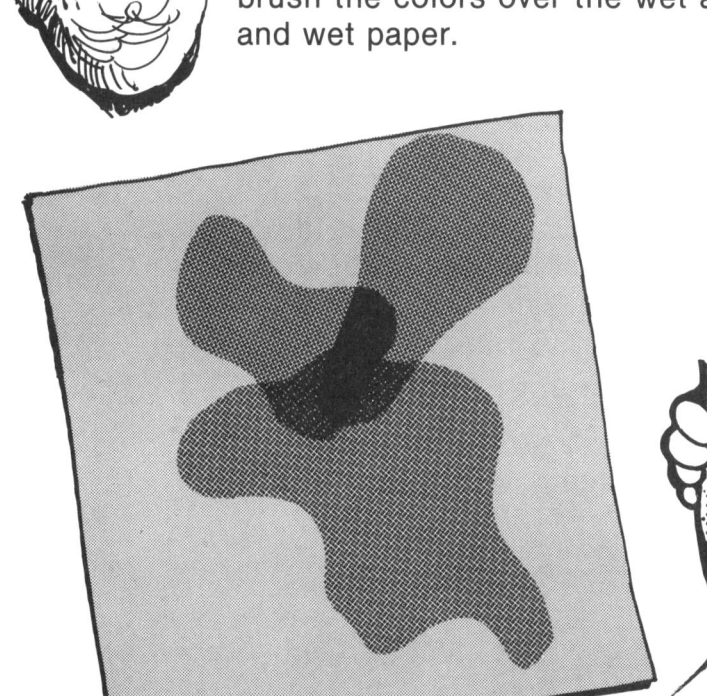

• Watercolors can also be used for mixing colors. Let the children mix them in paint pans, tins or on their papers using a water wash. Wet the paper thoroughly with a wet brush; then brush the colors over the wet area. Compare using dry paper and wet paper.

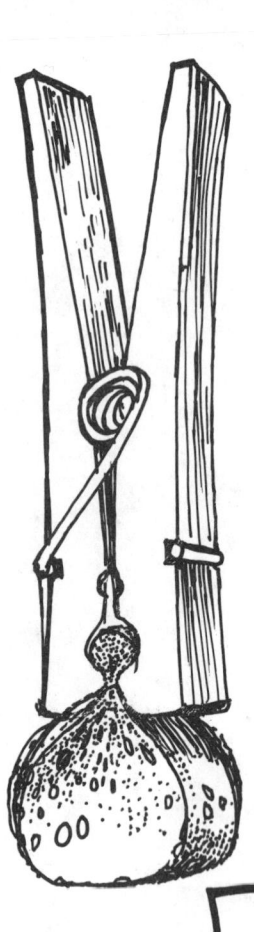

# Spongy Trees

**MATERIALS:**

- tempera paint—yellow, red and orange
- sponges—cut into 1" square pieces
- egg cartons—cut into sections of 4
- clip-type clothespins
- brown construction paper
- scissors
- glue
- 9" x 12" construction paper

Tree Trunk—
Cut 1

**PROCEDURE:**

1. Reproduce the tree trunk pattern. Cut it out and trace it onto oaktag. On brown construction paper trace and cut out one trunk for each child. Older children can trace and cut out their own trunks, or they may want to design their own.

2. Prepare paint for each work area.

3. Cut the sponges into 1" pieces. Dampen them and wring out any excess water. Clip one clothespin to the sponge piece to make a handle.

4. Cut the brown construction paper into 3" x 3" pieces.

5. Pass out one piece of white construction paper and tree trunk to each child.

6. Each child will glue his tree trunk to his piece of white construction paper.
7. Each child will use the sponges to dab paint around the trunk to make fall leaves.

**OTHER SUGGESTIONS:**

• This project can be done in the spring by substituting the red, orange and yellow paint with pink, white and lavender.

• To get the children to experiment with the dabbing method of painting desired for this project, you can do a practice project before actually tackling the trees. Prepare the practice project in the same manner as the above project. Demonstrate the different ways of moving the sponge across the paper. Discuss with the children what the various results are. Let them compare and contrast the strokes you have made. Let them try to produce different types of strokes using their own sponges. Talk about which strokes look most like leaves, flowers, clouds, waves, etc. Remind them of this practice project as you begin work on the trees.

• Cut the sponges into the shapes of different varieties of leaves.

• Use tissue paper or pieces of colored confetti to make the leaves instead of paint.

• On blue paper paint black stems. Using sponges and white or gray paint, make pussy willows. Use yellow paint to make spring forsythia. Colored soap flakes moistened to a paint consistency will also work.

# Inky Spiderwebs

**MATERIALS:**

- India ink—any color

- 8 1/2" x 11" paper—a nonabsorbent kind, like ditto paper. DO NOT USE CONSTRUCTION PAPER!

- plastic drinking straws (Paper straws will also work, but the plastic straws will last longer.)

- black construction paper

- small tie wraps from garbage bags

**PROCEDURE:**

1. Reproduce the spider pattern provided. Cut it out and trace it onto oaktag. Use this pattern to trace one spider for each child. Older children can trace and cut out the pieces themselves. They may also want to try to cut the shapes freehand.
2. Give each child one piece of 8 1/2" x 11" paper and a drinking straw.
3. Walk around the work area and drop a small amount of ink onto each child's paper. Each child will blow the ink around on his paper with the straw. Add more ink to each paper as needed. Use your discretion and give suggestions to the children if they still have enough ink on their papers. For example, "I think you missed this spot of ink on the top of your paper. Can you blow it around some more?"
4. When each child has an interesting pattern on his paper, set it aside to dry. Pass out 1 spider shape and 8 tie wraps to each child.
5. Each child will glue one end of each tie wrap to the edge of the spider's body. Put 4 tie wraps on each side.
6. When the glue on the legs has dried, bend the tie wraps to look like spider legs. Glue the spider onto its inky web.

**OTHER SUGGESTIONS:**

• Many of the ink bottles manufactured today have droppers made of a more brittle plastic which will crack with repeated squeezing. To make this project more successful, save the eyedroppers from children's liquid aspirin and clean them thoroughly. These droppers hold more ink, are more elastic and will not crack.

• This project is a good one for an insect unit or after a nature walk. What other kinds of insects can you make?

• Find a real spiderweb. Spray it with paint. Gently lay a piece of paper onto the spray-painted side. This is best done outside. Finish as above.

• Use fluorescent paint or ink to make the spiderweb for an eery glow-in-the-dark feeling for Halloween.

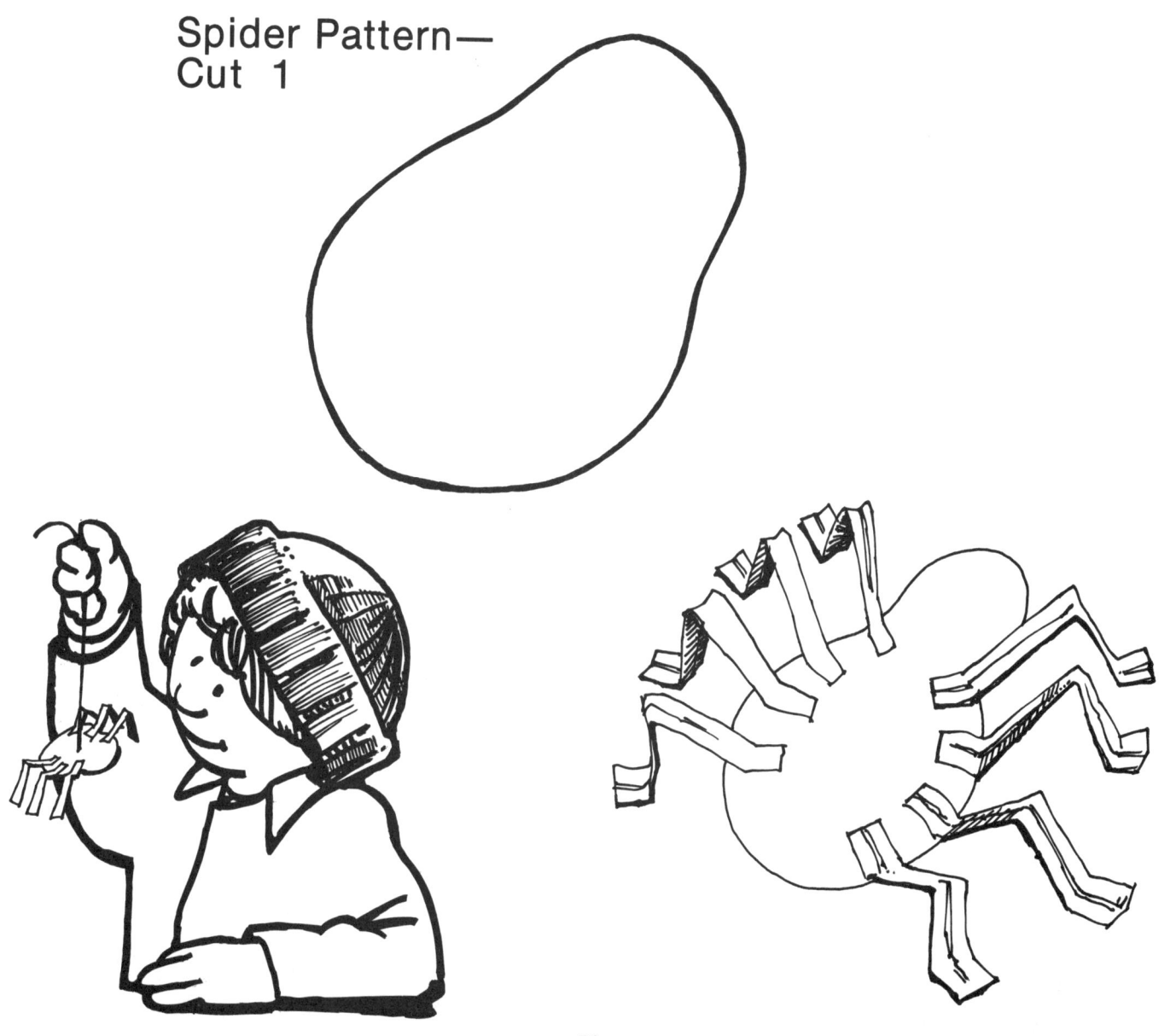

Spider Pattern—
Cut 1

# Frosty Fingers

**MATERIALS:**

- several packages of instant vanilla pudding
- construction paper—bright colors
- newspapers to cover desks or tables
- a spoon of some type

**PROCEDURE:**

1. Prepare the pudding according to the instructions.
2. Cover the desks or tables being used with newspaper.
3. Pass out one piece of brightly colored construction paper to each child.
4. Using a serving spoon, dollop a small amount of pudding onto each child's paper.
5. Let the children explore the texture, consistency and flow of the pudding on their papers. Encourage them to make movements using just their fingers. Let the children explore the types of movements they can make. Add pudding to the papers as needed.
6. Set the paintings aside to dry. When they are dry, mount them on white paper to display.

**OTHER SUGGESTIONS:**

- For some interesting fun, tell the children to put their hands behind their backs and put the pudding on their papers. Tell them you have added a new rule today—they may not use their hands. At first they will respond with uncertainty, but soon one of the braver children will discover the tongue works wonderfully. You'll soon have a roomful of painters painting with a tasty medium.

• To produce an interesting effect, you can color the pudding rainbow colors and paint on white paper. Let each child choose the color he prefers to work with. Do the project in the same manner as on the preceding page. When the pictures have dried, mount them on paper that matches the pudding to display them.

• This project can also be done using soap flakes that have been mixed with water and whipped or with shaving cream that has had a few drops of food coloring added for color. Don't try using tongues here!

# Easy Christmas Wreaths

**MATERIALS:**

- large construction paper
- tempera paint—green (red is optional)
- scissors
- glue
- disposable pie tins
- newspaper to cover the desks or worktables

**PROCEDURE:**

1. Reproduce the bow pattern. Cut it out and trace onto oaktag. Cut out the oaktag pattern and trace the bow onto red paper. Cut out enough bows for each child in your class. Older children can trace and cut out the pattern themselves. You can also let older children experiment with making 3-D bows.

2. Cover the work area with newspaper.

3. Prepare the paint. Pour the green paint into pie tins. Put only enough to cover the bottoms of the pans and prepare one of each color for each student or for every other student depending on class size and the ability of the children in the class to work together.

4. On the large piece of construction paper, trace a circle about 12" wide. Trace another inside it about 7" wide. When you are done drawing the circles, the paper should look like a large doughnut has been drawn on it.

5. Pass out the tins of green paint and the pieces of large white paper on which circles have been traced.

6. Let the children dip their hands into the tins of paint so that their palms are covered. Roll up any long sleeves for this step! Each child will press his hand down on the paper between the two circles that are drawn with his fingers apart and pointing to the outside of the doughnut.
7. Let the children keep printing until their wreaths are filled with handprints.
8. When the wreaths have a nice full look, hang or set them aside to dry.
9. When the wreaths are dry, each child will glue the red bow to the bottom of his wreath.
10. Let each child cut around the outside edge of the largest circle.
11. On the inside of the wreath add a Christmas greeting or poem and the child's signature. The children have created Christmas decorations parents will cherish for years to come.

**OTHER SUGGESTIONS:**

• Use construction paper instead of paint to make the handprints.

• Go to your local pizzeria and ask for small pizza circles. (Most places are willing to donate these.) Cover these with Christmas paper. Continue by using paint or construction paper to make the wreath. Finish the project as stated above.

• Use real ribbon or yarn to make the bow. Add red glitter to make sparkly berries. Or make the bow from two red handprints made with paint; berries can be made from fingerprints and red paint or ink.

# Bottoms-Up Butterflies

**MATERIALS:**

- tempera paint—any color or assorted colors
- 9" x 12" white construction paper
- disposable pie tins (large enough to put tiny feet in)
- a bucket of warm soapy water
- a sunny and mild day when you can be outside
- newspaper or an old plastic tablecloth

**PROCEDURE:**

1. Pour paint into the pie tins.
2. Prepare the bucket of water.
3. Anchor newspapers or an old plastic tablecloth to the ground or sidewalk where you will paint.
4. Take your class outside for a time of supervised play. While the children are playing, bring a small group of children (4-5) over to the paint area. Have them take their shoes and socks off and line up behind the tins of paint.
5. Set out one tin of paint for each child and let him stand behind it. Put a piece of construction paper on the other side of his tin. Place a bucket of warm soapy water on the far side of the paper. Set up the equipment for each child in the group in this manner. On the count of 3 let the children all step into their tins of paint and onto their papers. Have them step into their buckets of clean soapy water to clean up. Provide towels to dry their feet and help the group put their shoes and socks back on. Help anyone who needs assistance. Prepare for the next small group.

6. After the play period is over, take the kids and the dry footprints inside. Let the children cut out the shapes their feet made on the paper.
7. Take the two painted footprints and glue them close together onto a contrasting color of construction paper. Let each child add scraps of paper to make a body for the butterfly and provide two halves of a pipe cleaner to make antennae.

**OTHER SUGGESTIONS:**

• Make four prints of the child's hand to make a butterfly.

• After the wings have been glued down and have dried, let the children paint a pattern on each wing. The patterns can be from the children's imagination, or you can provide examples and pictures of real butterflies for the students to copy.

• Using string, paint a 9" x 12" piece of paper with various colors. Dip the string into the paint and lay it on the paper. Repeat until the paper is full of squiggly designs. When the paint is dry, trace the children's feet and finish as above.

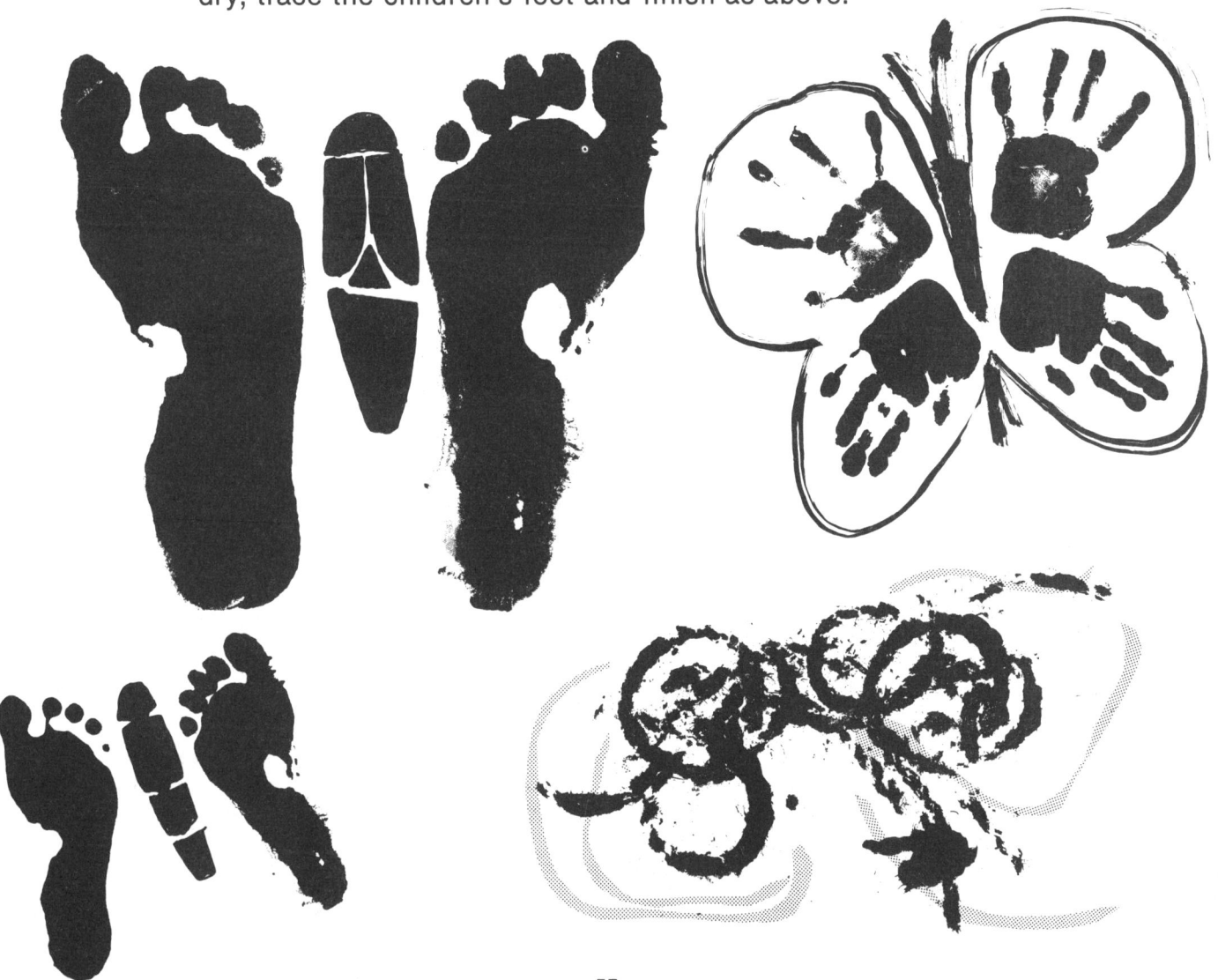

# Collage

Children like nothing better than using materials in different ways. Collages can be a fun way to experiment with new ways to use a variety of materials. Provide a large variety of materials for a project or at an art center for the children to use to create something uniquely their own. For motivation, use some of the drawing activities found on page 8 of this book or think up some of your own and add them to the page for future reference. You will find that once you have given the students a mountain of material, an idea, gobs of glue and the freedom to create in the classroom environment, they will really come up with some amazing creations!

Don't throw anything away! Keep collecting items that will keep your art center well-stocked with loads of interesting bits and pieces. Following are some suggestions of things to collect:

| | |
|---|---|
| baking papers | egg cartons |
| seeds | beans |
| scraps of yarn | scraps of material |
| pieces of wood | paper napkins |
| styrofoam cups (of various size) | buttons |
| | straw |
| string of all kinds | ribbon |
| wallpaper samples | magazines |
| old photos | cancelled stamps |
| sawdust | pieces of foam rubber |
| sandpaper | postcards |
| gift wrap | old greeting cards |
| labels | wrappers from candy, gum, etc. |
| pebbles | |
| twigs | sand |
| | styrofoam peanuts |

If your storage space is limited, ask parents to save these items for you. Let them bring the items to school when they don't have room for more at home or send a note home one week in advance asking for the items you will need. Specify the date you will need them.

# Things to Do with Seeds and Beans

- Make shapes, letters and numbers by gluing them to paper.

- Write your name.

- Trace a stencil using the patterns found on pages 16-19. Glue seeds or beans around the edges and fill in the shapes with other seeds or beans. Do this on paper, cardboard or pieces of wood.

- Put several bottles of glue and a large number of seeds and beans at the art center with a number of papers that have simple, bold outlines on them (like coloring book pages). Let the children "color" their pages by gluing the seeds and beans to them.

- To give a dot-to-dot paper a new twist, let the student glue beans and seeds to the paper to connect the dots. Color the picture after the glued-on outline has dried. Colored rice or popcorn kernels work well for this activity, too.

- Let older children create mosaics using the seeds and beans. This can be done by gluing seeds and beans to almost any of the cut-and-paste projects found in this book.

# Things to Do with Clay

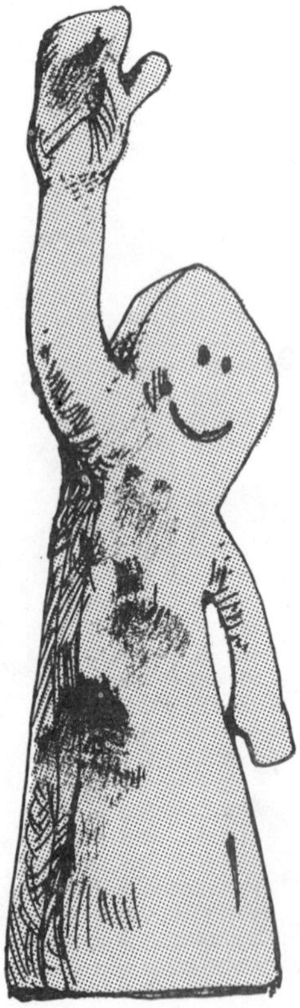

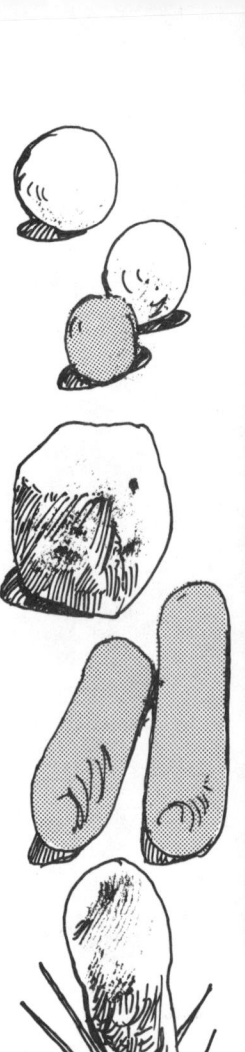

Clay is a fun medium to use with children. They love to bend, stretch, pull, pinch and roll clay into balls. For teachers, clay can be a great tool for helping develop fine motor skills. Here are some ideas to consider when using clay.

• Give the students as many different kinds of clay as you can think of to experiment with. There are many available.

   Play-Doh
   plasticene
   potter's clay
   modeling clay
   clay dug from a riverbed
   salt dough
   homemade

Here is an excellent recipe for homemade play dough that works well.

### PLAY DOUGH

Mix together in bowl:
   2 c. flour
   2 tbsp. alum

Heat to boiling:
   1 1/2 c. water
   1/2 c. salt
   1 tbsp. oil
   food coloring

Stir liquids into dry ingredients. Knead until smooth. Store in airtight container.

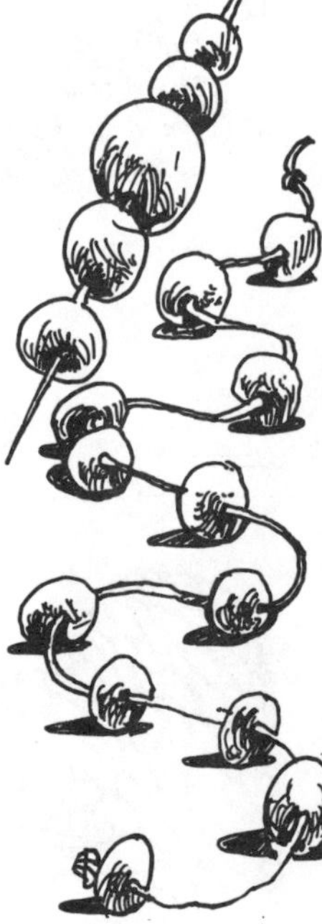

• Cut clay with scissors.

• Cut clay with cookie cutters.

• Roll clay into balls. Use toothpicks or pipe cleaners to make sculptures. Colored toothpicks add a little more fun.

• Roll clay into small bead-sized balls. Gently push onto toothpicks. Set aside to dry. When dry remove from toothpicks. Decorate and string on yarn for necklaces or bracelets.